The Art of
Thank You

The Art of Thank You

CRAFTING NOTES OF GRATITUDE

Connie Leas

ATRIA BOOKS
New York London Toronto Sydney

BEYOND WORDS
PUBLISHING

ATRIA BOOKS

A Division of Simon & Schuster, Inc.
1230 Avenue of the Americas
New York, NY 10020

BEYOND WORDS
PUBLISHING

20827 N.W. Cornell Road, Suite 500
Hillsboro, Oregon 97124-9808
tel: 503-531-8700 fax: 503-531-8773
www.beyondword.com

Editor: Jenefer Angell
Mangaging Editors: Julie Steigerwaldt and Lindsay S. Brown
Proofreader: Marvin Moore
Design: Starletta Polster and Susan Stutz
Composition: William H. Brunson Typography Services

First Atria Books/Beyond Words hardcover edition May 2007

ATRIA BOOKS and colophon are trademarks of Simon & Shuster, Inc. Beyond Words Publishing is a division of Simon & Schuster, Inc.

For information about special discounts for bulk purchases, please contact Simon & Schuster Special Sales at 1-800-456-6798 or business@simonandschuster.com

Manufactured in the United States of America

10 9 8 7 6 5 4 3

Library of Congress Control Number: 2001056559
ISBN-13:   978-1-58270-077-9
ISBN-10:   1-58270-077-X

The corporate mission of Beyond Words Publishing Inc.:
Inspire to Integrity

*The deepest principle in human nature
is the craving to be appreciated.*
—William James

To the Reader

Dear Readers:

Thank you for selecting this book—or for taking a look at it. I hope you find it useful and inspiring—even entertaining.

I came up with the idea of writing a thank-you-note book after a wedding gift I had sent was not acknowledged. In trying to imagine the reasons for this breach of etiquette, I concluded that the recipients of my gift either didn't know that a gift requires a thank-you— which is hard to believe—or that they felt insecure about their note-writing skills. Either way, I decided a how-to book was in order.

I started out by going to the library and checking out all the etiquette books available—usually very large tomes that covered everything from how to set a table to proper behavior on the tennis court. I also scoured magazines, newspapers, and the Internet. Little by little, I became something of a thank-you-note expert.

My early drafts focused rather narrowly on rules, etiquette, and social correctness, as well as on the dire consequences of neglecting to write thank-you notes—

a sort of verbal finger wagging. However, the longer I stuck with it—the more I read and the more people I talked to—I found more and more examples of thoughtfulness and kindness motivated not by the "oughts" and "shoulds" of social convention but by an empathetic regard for the feelings of others. Little by little, themes of generosity, gratitude, kindness, and consideration took up a larger share of the book—and rightfully so.

I am no thank-you-note poster child. My notes are not as beautifully written as many of those you'll find in this book and I don't offer them as freely as do some of the people you'll meet here. Also, I didn't work as hard to train my children as the parents mentioned in these pages. But I will take credit for introducing you to these remarkable people and for sharing the memorable thank-you notes I've collected.

It appears that thank-you notes are on the decline, a consequence, I suspect, of the electronic gadgetry that has made us impatient with activities requiring time and effort. As expressions of gratitude diminish, so too do thoughtfulness and civility—virtues we can't afford to lose. Perhaps this book can help. So can you.

Connie Leas

Contents

Contents

Acknowledgments

I am not one who believes that too many cooks spoil the broth—at least not where the "broth" consists of a book like this one. I figure the more "cooks," the better. Many friends and relatives helped me by offering suggestions, opinions, criticisms, encouragement, ideas, thank-you notes, and anecdotes. Early on, when the book was just an idea, the enthusiasm of my daughter-in-law Cheryl Farr Leas—herself a writer—made me believe I should go ahead and write something. (Cheryl also offered valuable editorial assistance as well as thank-you notes, including the one from a Brooklyn firefighter.) My sister, Elaine Greensmith Jordan, alerted me to the Maui Writer's Conference Manuscript Service, without which I may never have found an agent and publisher. She also reviewed my earliest draft, offering suggestions that helped move the book toward its final form. So, too, did my friend Lucia Mouat, another writer.

I sent a later version of the manuscript to other friends and family, who reviewed it, corrected it, and offered suggestions for improvement. I am indebted to them for their attention to my project: Bob Good, Speed Leas, Bob MacKay, Kristi McKenzie, Karen Riechel, Jocelyn Stoody, Susan Thatcher, and Marion Weil. Another friend, Laura Dolson, put me in touch with Dawn Price, who writes daily thank-you notes—a great find!

Finally, thanks to my agent, Rita Rosenkranz, who, with unflagging attention, guided both the book and me toward publication; to my editor, Jenefer Angell, whose enthusiastic and cheerful approach to the project made collaboration a pleasure; and to my copy editor, Marvin Moore, whose perfectionism compensated for my lack thereof.

1

Kindness and Gratitude: Why We Write Thank-You Notes

Writing a thank-you note is a small but gracious way to repay kindness with kindness. By expressing gratitude in writing, you make sure others feel appreciated. Moreover, your note of thanks provides tangible evidence of your appreciation to the good people who have treated you well.

A thank-you note—especially one that is hand-written—is appreciated not only by gift-givers but by those who have hosted you for overnights, helped with a project, expressed condolences, done a good job, offered a sympathetic ear, found your lost wallet, invited you to dinner, lent you money, or any number of other generous acts. The list of possibilities is boundless. For example, an elderly man sent a thank-you note to the Internal Revenue Service expressing appreciation for their "fine young employee"; a grateful mother wrote Dr. Jonas Salk to thank him for developing the polio vaccine.

Usually we feel grateful to be on the receiving end of thoughtful acts; less often do we express our gratitude in writing. Cathy Keating, first lady of Oklahoma, is one person who writes her thanks, no matter how overwhelming the task. After the bombing of the Alfred P. Murrah Federal Office Building in Oklahoma City, she personally responded to the hundreds upon hundreds of offers of help, prayers, and money. It took her several

I am 84 and very Cranky-Fussy—

The Federal Income Tax Blanks get more complicated and hard to understand each year. I was sure I was not figuring correctly my Tax Report for those over 75 so I went down to your office-Room 1102 & secured help from young man in Help to Taxpayers office. I was very fussy and cranky after walking & Panting for 30 minutes but he was very patient with me & laughed me out of being mad. I was ashamed of myself. I asked for help in figuring on income & credits for those over 75. He made out my report & saved me $80.00.

Thank you & this fine young employee.

Old Man

I would guess that not many IRS employees receive thank-you notes. This one was saved and later published in Letters of the Century.

months to acknowledge each letter, but acknowledge them she did. "It was the right thing to do," she said. "Nothing can replace the acknowledgment of a kind deed better than a handwritten note from the heart."

Thank-you notes as treasures

For famous people, such as Jonas Salk, accolades may be commonplace, but you can be sure they are treasured nevertheless. For most of us, receiving a note of appreciation usually pleases us far beyond the expectations of the note-writer. In fact, notes of thanks attain an almost trophy-like status and are often saved and displayed.

My mechanic has tacked a collection of smudged and faded thank-you notes to the walls of his grimy office. Doctors also save their notes of thanks. In an editorial in *Patient Care* journal, Dr. Karl Singer writes that he saves expressions of thanks in a special file. "They're a counterbalance to the inevitable complaints, negative reviews, and lawsuits that we all get at some time or another as physicians." Dr. Singer also tells of a "note" he received in the form of a large cake on which was written "Thanks Dr. Singer and staff for 25 years of great care." "That day," he reports, "everyone in the office felt happy." One rural doctor, Kathryn

April 13, 1955

Dear Doctor Salk—

Not the least among the many honors a grateful world bestows upon you are the blessings of a million mothers to whom your discovery means freedom from a most tragic fear. When I realize that my young daughter and another child as yet unborn will never suffer from polio, I am more grateful than words can express to you and to all the others who have made this possible.

Most sincerely,
Joanna H. Shurbet

Some people, like this mother writing to express her thanks to Dr. Jonas Salk, don't keep their gratitude to themselves. They are an inspiration.

5

Rensenbrink, after visiting the home of a dying patient, received a letter from the man's daughter, thanking the doctor "for coming like a guardian spirit out of the winter dark." "How wonderful," Dr. Rensenbrink writes, "to be most appreciated when you feel the least able."

Ministers especially treasure notes of thanks. One minister says he saves his thank-yous in a file under "E" for "encouragement." He pulls them out "on those days you think you should resign." Another pastor reports that such notes give him the "assurance that my work is not in vain."

Especially worthy of praise are those people who write thank-yous to gladden the hearts of strangers who have provided a valued service. My daughter-in-law, who writes travel guides, has received thank-yous from people who appreciate her well-researched recommendations of hotels and restaurants. Like many of us, she saves and prizes such notes, which may serve as the only evidence that her work has value to others. "I'm always so thrilled when readers write thank-you notes," Cheryl says. "Most readers don't think about the people who do the intensive work that goes into writing an annual travel guide. So when somebody takes the time and energy to say thank you, I know that I've really connected with them on a personal level. That's what makes it all worthwhile."

Dear Elaine,

I was so happy to talk with you the other night... This whole experience has been so healing for Kathy and I but on different levels... I always felt I had a sister. I am so happy. We have bonded so quickly. It's been a blessing in both of our lives. It's almost like being born again.

I've always been so terribly depressed on my birthday but this year I think I'm starting to feel differently. I'm starting to feel whole for the first time in my life... The pain in my heart is gone after 42 years. Without your interview and letter to 'The Village' I would have never found my sister!

You are loved,
Wendy

My sister, Elaine Greensmith Jordan, received this note from a friend whom she had helped in locating adoption information.

Happiness shared

Thank-you notes not only make us feel appreciated, they also allow us to experience the good feelings we engender by our thoughtful acts. This notion hadn't occurred to me until I read a story by Roxana Robinson in *The New York Times Magazine* titled "Great Expectations: Should an Act of Kindness Merit Something in Return?" In the article she tells of finding a wallet in a cab, locating the owner's phone number, and calling to tell him she had found his wallet. Instead of hearing ecstatic statements of relief and gratitude, she heard only a calm "Oh good. Thank you." He said little more except "I will pick it up tomorrow." Ms. Robinson was disappointed. She wanted to "talk about how wonderful it all was." Later she consoled herself, thinking he would surely leave a "grateful note" or a "heartfelt message on our machine."

She left the wallet with her doorman, and the owner picked it up, but he left no note in return. Days passed. Ms. Robinson began analyzing her feelings: "At first I was disappointed, but by evening I felt foolish. Why had I expected a deluge of gratitude? I had felt so noble, but in fact I hadn't been noble at all, only responsible. My entire effort had cost exactly 25 cents.

Karen,

Thank you very much for that rather hefty graduation present. I hope Aimee knows how lucky she is to have a mother as kind and outgoing as yourself. Since I'm still going to be around, you're welcome to interject with any motherly advice anytime you hear my mom giving me a lecture before I go out.

Thanks again,
Chris Medley

A friend of mine received the following note of thanks from a youthful neighbor to whom she had given a graduation check. As with so many notes of thanks, my friend appreciated and enjoyed it so much that she saved it.

Why had I expected to be treated like a hero? . . . I was embarrassed by my own expectations."

Four days after finding the wallet, Ms. Robinson received an orchid with a card that said, "Thank you. Thank you. Thank you. I love New York!" The wallet owner was clearly grateful, and Ms. Robinson was surely gratified by his gift and note. And while the opportunity to talk about "how wonderful it all was" had passed, the note of thanks conveyed his delight in having his wallet returned.

We can all identify with the author's expectations as she called the owner of the wallet and waited for—but didn't receive—his enthusiastically happy response. If we have made others happy, we want the feeling to wash over us. A thank-you note can make it happen.

I suspect the desire to share the happiness may be the reason doctors, who often receive gifts as expressions of gratitude, would much prefer a thank-you note, even if the gifts are extremely valuable. (The former Shah of Iran used to give Rolex watches.) Dr. Laura Popper, a New York City pediatrician, is a case in point. To save an infant who had stopped breathing, she ran from her office two and a half blocks to the parents' apartment. There she provided the resuscitation and follow-up measures that saved the child's life. Later, Dr. Popper received a box of

30 September 1959

Dear Mr. Marx:

Thanks for the book and for including my name at the end of that long, dreary list in the front. Thurber says it is alphabetical, but he is full of all sort of odd bits of information.

I'm enjoying the book, and it is one of the two books in my library in which the sentences seem to be uttered aloud by the author of the book. (The other book is Fred Allen's.)

My wife and I continue to watch your show with enjoyment, and the whole thing is better than ever now that the bittersweet vine has reached the top of our antenna, so that you come through the set looking more and more like Raymond Duncan, the goatherd. Keep up the good work, and tell Melinda I was enchanted with the witch doctor.

Sincerely,
E. B. White

Groucho Marx sent E. B. White, the well-known author of The Elements of Style, *a copy of his book* Groucho and Me. *White is mentioned in the acknowledgments.*

chocolates from the grateful parents. While she
appreciated the acknowledgment, she would have
appreciated even more a few words that described the
infant's return to health and the joy this brought the
parents. "I did care about the letter," she admitted—
that is, the one she didn't get.

Worldly rewards

Writing thank-you notes can be rewarding—sometimes extremely so. For example,

- Peter Cummings, chairman of the Detroit
  Symphony Orchestra, wrote a personal—and
  lengthy—thank-you note to an elderly heiress
  who had contributed $50,000 to the DSO. Two
  weeks later, the heiress contributed an additional
  $50,000. This pattern of donations followed by
  letters of gratitude continued until the DSO had
  received an unprecedented $2.5 million from
  this donor.

- A woman wrote to etiquette expert and columnist
  Miss Manners saying that her six-year-old
  "...writes her own notes and expresses delight
  in most gifts, even new toothbrushes, so it is fun
  to give her presents. Her grandmother and

godmother enjoy it so much, that they give her several gifts each month."

- A job-seeker was among five finalists for a highly desirable job. Of the five, she was the only one who sent a thank-you note following the interview. She got the job.
- A woman who had been shopping for a car received a personal letter of appreciation from just one of the eight or ten dealerships she visited. The dealer who wrote the note got her business. "I felt important and believed my business was truly wanted," she says.

On the other hand, failure to offer written thanks can be costly: grandmothers who do not receive thank-you notes have been known to cease gift giving.

Reputations in the balance

Failure to write a thank-you note can sully your reputation. If you received a gift, especially an expensive one, such as a wedding gift, and did not acknowledge it, your negligence will be remembered—and remembered for a long time. I read about a group of women who were gathered together in a spa hot tub, discussing regrets about unwritten letters. The topic prompted one participant to recall a bride and groom who, *fifty years ago*, neglected to acknowledge the gifts they'd received. "Nobody has forgotten it," she said.

I must admit that I, too, remember those people who did not send notes to acknowledge gifts I have sent—especially wedding and new-baby gifts. I know, from talking to friends, that others do too. When I don't receive a note, I tend to surmise that the recipient was never trained to do so, or is unsure of his or her writing skills, or has a problem with disorganization or procrastination. Some people who don't receive notes of acknowledgment may be less charitable than I, thinking, for example, that the non-note-writer is not grateful. (Andrè Comte-Sponville, author of *A Small Treatise on the Great Virtues*, defines the ungrateful person as one who is unable to give back "a little of the joy that was received or experienced.")

None of us wants to be remembered for negative reasons. Even if you are not otherwise motivated to express gratitude for a gift you have been given, the risk to your reputation should be motivation enough.

Justified grievances

People have a right to feel aggrieved at not receiving expressions of gratitude for gifts and other acts of kindness. Take, for example, the seventy-six-year-old grandmother who wrote to advice columnist Ann Landers, complaining that she receives no thanks from the fifty-two relatives to whom she regularly sends birthday and holiday gifts. The grandmother has clearly expended considerable time and effort on behalf of her relatives. In response, the relatives give nothing back: the gift is not followed by gratitude. While the relatives' neglect reflects poorly on them, of greater importance is the grandmother's feelings. For all of her efforts, the grandmother deserves some words of appreciation.

I like the way Miss Manners put it in her reply to the bride who complained that she wasn't able to write personal letters to all who sent gifts: "You can, by simply doing nothing, make it perfectly clear to all of your original and newly acquired relations and friends that the planning, shopping, and spending each has done on your account do not justify a two-minute effort and a stamp from you."

Real men write thank-you notes

Young men, I've learned, think that writing thank-you notes is not manly. When asked if he wrote thank-you notes, one twenty-three-year-old man replied, "I just don't think it's a thing that a guy has to do. I mean, the girls do it because it's a girl thing. But I feel kind of dorky doing it." It's "dorky" to express gratitude? A "girl thing" to write notes of thanks? Presidents Reagan, Carter, Clinton, G. H. Bush, and G. W. Bush are known for their handwritten notes. The writer Ernest Hemingway, a man's man if there ever was one, was also a regular writer of thank-you-notes. In fact, a hefty percentage of his letters began with "thank you." For example, here is a fragment of a thank-you letter he wrote to John and Katharine Dos Passos (January 13, 1936):

Thanks very much for the swell still champagne. The day it came Burris Jenkins was here with three other guys and we drank seven bottles. It was wonderful. Caught six sailfish the last six times out. Been feeling good again since about two weeks. Hope everything going well with youse.

If you're concerned about your manly reputation, then write a manly thank-you note. Like Hemingway, you can throw in something about the fish you caught or the bear you wrestled. But do write the note. I'll guarantee that the recipients will be both pleased and impressed, and your reputation will be burnished, not tarnished.

Dear Goldie,

Am I enchanted? You bet. Thanks for giving
me such a relaxed good time at dinner.
When Jane Weintraub told me where I was
sitting, I was a little worried *only* because I'm not
too hot of a dinner partner. (I didn't ask you to
dance—on that one, look at it this way—you've
still got 2 good feet.)
Anyway you were a fantastic dinner partner.
You made me feel welcome and totally at ease.
I didn't even have to unveil my 12-point plan for
dealing with Gorbachev. Thanks for being so
darn nice!!

Good Luck—
George Bush

*This note from President George H. Bush to Goldie
Hawn is a wonderful example of an expression of
gratitude not confined to the "when to send a thank-
you note" rules.*

Dear Madam,

I have been shown in the files of the War Department a statement of the Adjutant General of Massachusetts that you are the mother of five sons who have died gloriously on the field of battle. I feel how weak and fruitless must be any word of mine which should attempt to beguile you from the grief of a loss so overwhelming. But I cannot refrain from tendering to you the consolation that may be found in the thanks of the republic they died to save. I pray that our Heavenly Father may assuage the anguish of your bereavement, and leave you only the cherished memory of the loved and lost, and the solemn pride that must be yours to have laid so costly a sacrifice upon the altar of freedom.

Yours very sincerely and respectfully,
ALincoln

This famous letter to Mrs. Bixby of Boston, Massachusetts, offers thanks for the ultimate gift. The writer is Abraham Lincoln.

Consideration for others

While you may not feel you can rise to the heights of a perfect poem, common courtesy and consideration for the feelings of others demand that you always take the time to thank those who have spent time, money, or effort on your behalf. Even *Cosmopolitan* magazine includes writing thank-you notes as one of their "ten musts for daily life," along with getting in shape, not buying beyond your means, falling for a nice guy, and other "Cosmo commandments."

The notes you write demonstrate your thoughtfulness, good manners, and classiness. What's more, you'll find that expressing your gratitude in writing comes with a surprising level of personal satisfaction.

2

Occasions and Opportunities: When to Send Thank-You Notes

Thank-you notes are rarely inappropriate and are always appreciated by the recipient—sometimes profoundly so. A thank-you note is often the only reward people receive for special acts of kindness or a job well done. You can offer written thanks for just about anything—witness George H. Bush's note to Goldie Hawn thanking her for being such "a fantastic dinner partner." Although you're under no obligation to send a note of thanks to dinner partners—or to your mechanic, doctor, minister, librarian, or travel-guide writer—certain occasions absolutely require that you do so.

Musts, shoulds, and nice-tos

If your goal is simply to avoid social faux pas, then you can follow the rules provided by such etiquette experts as Letitia Baldrige, Emily and Peggy Post, and Judith Martin (Miss Manners). Bear in mind that rules of etiquette are not unreasonable dictates designed to force you against your will into socially correct behavior. Rather, they condition us to consider the feelings and sensibilities of others. Many of those oughts and shoulds we endured as children led us to civilized behavior as adults. Where thank-you notes are concerned, the goal is to respond to kindness with a kind word, generosity with expressions of gratitude, good deeds with a gesture of appreciation

All etiquette experts agree that you must absolutely send a written note of thanks for all wedding gifts and for other-occasion gifts for which you did not offer a verbal thanks. You should also send a note following an overnight stay as a guest in someone's home. Experts differ about the necessity to send notes for parties you attended, gifts for which you verbally thanked the giver, and a variety of other acts of kindness. All agree, however, that you can never go wrong sending a thank-you note.

Sometimes the decision to send a note will depend on the customs of your social set; the expectations of the giver; the degree of effort, time, or money expended by the giver; or your relationship to the giver. For example, Letitia Baldrige would have children write a thank-you note "after every meal at a friend's house." If that is how things are done in your neighborhood, then perhaps your child must adhere to this rigorous practice. But this was never done—or expected—in my social sphere. Similarly, if no one in your group of friends ever sends notes of thanks following dinner parties, then perhaps you needn't start this practice, although I guarantee your hosts would be pleased by your expression of gratitude.

Determining whether someone will be insulted by not receiving a note of thanks can sometimes be tricky because some givers have their own sliding scale of expectations. For example, one man, having loaned money to a friend on five occasions, felt OK about receiving only verbal thanks for the first four sums but thought he should have received a note for the last sum because it was considerably larger than the earlier ones. Peter Cummings, chairman of the Detroit Symphony Orchestra, has his own sliding scale for note writing. He writes personal notes to anyone who contributes more than $500 to the orchestra. Other contributors receive form letters.

Of course, in trying to determine if a thank-you note is appropriate, you can simply follow your better instincts and send a note of appreciation in response to any notable act of kindness. If you nevertheless seek guidance on the musts, oughts, and nice-tos of thank-you-note writing, I offer the following suggestions. (For a quick reference, see the table in the appendix.)

Social occasions

Some of the occasions listed below are those for which thank-you notes are required—at least according to conventional notions of good manners and

February 21, 1937

Dear Miss Crane,

It is well I did not know when I received the mysterious box, that a nautilus was inside, or my hand might have shaken so as to injure it. A nautilus has always seemed to me something supernatural. The more I look at it the less I can credit it,—this large yet weightless thing, with a glaze like ivory on the entrance and even on the sides. How curious the sudden change of direction in the corrugations, and the transparent oyster white dullness of the "paper." The wings are so symmetrical I should not know any part had been broken if you had not said so....

Mother takes as much pleasure in the nautilus as I do, and was so impressed with the beauty of the wrappings, my opening of the box and the envelope, was considerably delayed.

Affectionately yours, Marianne M.

Poet Marianne Moore, in a letter to a friend, Louise Crane, gets the prize for "mention what you like about the gift," which, in this case, was a shell.

commonsense thoughtfulness. For other occasions, consider the feelings of the recipient and let your conscience be your guide.

Following the receipt of wedding gifts

People who send wedding gifts deserve a written note of thanks, regardless of whether the gifts were mailed, hand-carried, or even opened in front of the giver with an expression of thanks. You must write a note—no excuses. One couple tried to get out of writing notes by including the following in their newspaper wedding announcement: "In lieu of sending personal thank-you notes for wedding gifts, the couple made a donation to the American Cancer Society." How, I ask myself, does donating to a charity begin to substitute for thanking the good people who sent gifts to this couple?

Just as the bride and groom expect gifts, so the gift-givers expect a note of thanks. As Miss Manners says, generosity and gratitude go hand in hand. If you want to avoid writing notes of appreciation, then insist on a no-gifts wedding.

Following the receipt of gifts on other occasions

Naturally, a gift warrants your thanks, either verbally or in writing. For example, if you receive a gift by mail and did not call to thank the giver, then a thank-you

Dear Ernestine,

Unfortunately, this letter is the third one I've written this evening, so it probably won't be as long as I had intended, since I get tired of typing and thinking.

Thank you for the dress! I'm wearing it right now. It's just what I needed (as you had guessed) for after I get cleaned up in the evening. And I've been getting pretty dirty lately, since we've been painting the outside of the house and digging a ditch from the pump house to the barn (we're putting water in the barn for winter use). The dress is a perfect fit—even the length is perfect. Speed says it's just like being married to a girl....

For ten years, we lived on a farm in Michigan. My mother-in-law saved all the letters I had sent her from this "back to the land" period in our lives. This example shows just the first two paragraphs of a letter in which I thanked her for a sort of lounging dress she sent me for my birthday. The reference to "Speed," as you would guess, is to my husband.

note is in order. Still better, send a thank-you note even if you did offer a verbal thanks. Some etiquette experts believe that every gift must be acknowledged in writing—not just by a telephone call. I say you can use your judgment here. If you know that Grandma is satisfied with a phone call and uses the phone herself to express thanks, then perhaps the call is sufficient. If, however, you know that Grandma expects a note—or would be especially pleased at receiving a note—then send a note. Always send a note if the gift represents an especially generous amount of time or money, such as a handmade quilt or season tickets to the opera. One young woman received a gold bracelet from her grandmother and had thanked Grandma several times in person and later on the phone, but she did not send a note, thinking such a gesture would be overdoing it. She was wrong—Grandma later reprimanded her for not having sent a thank-you note.

Etiquette experts disagree on whether or not children should write thank-you notes for gifts they receive at their birthday parties. Letitia Baldrige says they should; Judith Martin says it's not necessary, unless the gift is "extremely serious." I would side with Martin. As always, however, a thank-you note is always welcome and may even be expected. Of course, if the birthday child receives a gift from someone who

My Dearest Abigail,

I was so moved by your generous hospitality on my recent visit that I just had to sit down immediately and compose this modest and woefully inadequate note of thanks. As usual, I was welcomed with opened arms and treated royally. Your house looked lovely, and you truly outdid yourself with my arrival brunch of fresh strawberries, poached eggs, and homemade biscuits. Dinner that night was a feast for the eyes and the palate. The fresh garden squash and butterbeans were colorful complements to the chicken and wild rice.

I think it is marvelous how you young people have learned that baked is healthier than fried, and how you have made that transition losing hardly any of the taste. The pecan and peach pies were delicious as I, again, could not force myself to choose just one. The Continental-style breakfast the next morning was charming and really all I desired before my drive home.

Thank you once again for letting me come visit. I thoroughly enjoyed my stay and hope to repeat the trip soon.

> Much love and warm regards,
> Aunt Eulalah

This note, written by Joe Kropp (not "Aunt Eulalah") in the Southern Journal, *illustrates for him the Southern thank-you notes, which, he says, "read more like journal entries, chronicling not only the receiving of some kind of gesture, but also detailing the very texture of each strand woven into the fabric of the moment." In the Southern style, he says,* thoroughly *must precede the word* enjoy, *and* treated *must be followed by* royally.

Dear Connie and Speed,

Am feeling very embarrassed that my "B & B" letter has been so long delayed! Miss Manners would say "no excuses," and there aren't any! Just lazy lingering remembrances of what a splendid several days it was, and of how full all of my senses are; a savoring that I don't want to put an end to! I can make "*the list,*" (incredible house, leisurely tours, an abundance of your time and undivided attention, great sights and sounds and tastes, a fabulous game plan, incredible organization, airline tickets [!], deep sleeps) but none of these things takes the "thank you" priority.

What I am actually cherishing the most is the pleasure of having friends of over twenty years who I have known through so many seasons of life; friends who—although we now have rather minimal contact—I still count among my nearest and dearest, and with whom I still feel absolutely comfortable and delighted to be with; with whom I can spend five days and still be sad to leave.

It was wonderful to be on your "new turf"; to share yet another venue. I truly do love the house! I love the design, I love the use of space and the sense that internal and external blend, I love the site and vistas, I love the comfort of it, and I love

how much it absolutely reflects the two of you and
sort of sums up who you are and what's important
to you. It felt like you had been there always; it
felt like home.

Mostly, I love the two of you. What else is there
to say? Thank you for all you do to continue to
bring us together! I feel very blessed! Bless you!

> Love,
> Kristi

*I have received some wonderful thank-you notes from
non-Southerners that also read like "journal entries."
This note, from my friend Kristi McKenzie, is one
example. (The original was actually longer; I
removed a paragraph of reminiscences.) "B and B,"
by the way, means "bread and butter"—an old-
fashioned term for notes written in response to
hospitality.*

was unable to attend the party, a thank-you note should be sent. The same holds true in cases where the birthday child did not open the gifts at the party. (See chapter 7 for more information on children and thank-you notes.)

Adults should write thank-you notes for presents received in a party setting, such as for birthday and anniversary celebrations. In such settings, when the guest of honor is opening gift after gift, expressions of gratitude are generally brief, even if enthusiastic. I attended a surprise party in which the guest of honor was showered with gifts for her new apartment. After the party, I found myself hoping that she'd write a note to let me know how well she liked the gift. She did. While I certainly didn't feel it was her duty to do so, or even that it was the polite thing to do—after all, she'd thanked me when she opened the gift—I was pleased to receive a more personal word of appreciation for the effort and money I spent on her behalf.

Following an overnight stay as the guest of others

A thank-you note following an overnight stay in someone's home is an etiquette standard. After all, when you weigh the chores of cooking, cleaning, and entertaining against the chore of writing a letter, a letter is not too much to ask. Peggy Post makes an exception "in the case of close friends or relatives whom you see frequently." Then, she says, "a telephone call would serve the purpose." (As far as I'm concerned, writing a note is usually easier, less time-consuming, and less bothersome to the hosts than a phone call.) Children who have been treated by others to a special trip or an extended stay should also write thank-yous.

Following parties and dinners hosted by others

Some of my friends always send thank-you notes following dinner parties. Others do not. Sometimes I do; sometimes I don't. Whether or not you send a note depends on the habits of your social set and the formality of the occasion. For example, we don't send notes after the meals we eat at the home of one set of friends because we get together regularly, taking turns hosting the meal—and neither of us expects it. On the other hand, we have other friends who always send a note after dining in our home, and I always welcome their flattering words of appreciation—and take note of the writer's good manners and thoughtfulness.

Etiquette experts are divided on the need to write thank-you notes following parties. Some believe that written thank-yous are required; for others, notes are optional. However, all agree that you must send a note

Dear Connie and Speed,

Thank you so much for your impromptu storm-gathering and dinner invitation. It was so thoughtful of you to think of us and to provide such a wonderful dinner, a "clean well-lighted" and warm house, excellent camaraderie and lots of good humor!

As usual, your black-bean soup and "fixings" were delicious, and the whole table was gorgeous with your new Mexican dishes.

We were so happy to inaugurate them!

Here's hoping Thursday's storm is not as challenging.

Mil gracias,
Carolyn and Leo

The occasion for this note was an impromptu dinner I threw together one night when most everyone in town lost electricity. Because we have a generator, we were able to maintain the comforts. The writer is a friend, Carolyn McKenna, who always sends a nice note after every meal in our home. She is an inspiration.

of thanks following special parties, such as formal dinners or elaborate meals. A note is also required for parties at which you were the guest of honor, such as a wedding rehearsal or anniversary dinner.

For special acts of kindness

It's always nice to write a note of gratitude for special kindnesses, such as after someone has treated you to a concert, written a letter of reference on your behalf, helped you move, hosted your baby shower, rescued your dog, or loaned you a car. (Letitia Baldrige would even have you write a thank-you note to a friend who takes you to the movies.) Brides and grooms should write notes of thanks to all who helped with the wedding, including members of the wedding party as well as anyone else who assisted with the wedding, such as friends who hosted out-of-town wedding guests.

People sometimes wonder if it's necessary or proper to acknowledge the receipt of preprinted cards, such as Easter cards or get-well cards. While you needn't feel obliged to send a response to such cards, sending a brief message on a postcard acknowledges this expression of goodwill. In response to those who have sent get-well cards, you can thank the senders when you meet or speak by phone.

I owe you so much for caring for me;
Without you I'd be camped 'neath a tree.
There're items I'd buy, but which would it be?
The list looks like Christmas—I dream it with glee.
A dog who doesn't chase cows would be nice,
Or a year's worth of bandages for knees that need ice.
Cookies and tea for all of our ills
And loads of money for high doctor bills.
But not one of those could come close to the fee
I owe you IN LOVE, which at your house is free.
You fed me, and kept me out of straits dire;
You drew me a lion; you fixed my flat tire.
You carried my stuff; you took me to sales
In garages with bargains in bonnets and pails!
You told me good stories before I retired
And even were generous with your clothes dryer.
You both were just perfect, like Mom and like
Dad; so . . .
I've made a decision I hope you'll find glad.
I can't bear to leave you, next Friday, I think—
So I'll send the trucks back and stay under the sink.

Here's a thank-you poem my sister wrote to the family
with whom she stayed while she was waiting for
escrow to close on her new home.

To acknowledge good service and helpfulness

You can make someone's day by writing a thank-you letter to or about the often-neglected people who come to your rescue, including employees of businesses, such as airline flight attendants, and governmental employees, such as firefighters. For example, if an airline employee was exceptionally helpful, or if the rescue squad competently handled a life-threatening situation, a thank-you letter ensures that these people get the credit they deserve. In such cases, you should send the letter to the president of the company or to the head of the organization, who, it's presumed, would see to it that the letter goes into the person's personnel file.

You can also acknowledge good service by writing letters of thanks to those who succeeded in solving a problem about which others may have given you the runaround. For example, by sending a thank-you note to the person who finally solves your problem with Social Security or a credit card, you not only reward their act of kindness, you encourage them to keep up the good work, and thus improve service for everyone!

Of course, it is especially thoughtful to send a note of thanks to anyone, stranger or not, who has helped you in any way. Notes such as these are guaranteed to make the recipient happy.

Following a funeral

Following a funeral, you should send a note of thanks to those who sent flowers, charitable contributions in memory of the deceased, and condolence letters or telegrams. (Even though charities send notes of thanks to the donor, you should also send one.) You should also send notes of appreciation to the person who directed the proceedings, the clergyperson who handled the service, pallbearers and ushers, speakers (if not family members), and those who provided food. Bear in mind, however, that the notes can be written by anyone in the family and needn't be sent immediately.

While some etiquette experts would have you write notes of thanks to anyone who sent a sympathy card (as distinguished from a letter of condolence), others would not strictly require it. Preworded acknowledgment cards, such as those that say "The family of [deceased's name] greatly appreciates your kind expression of sympathy" are fine in exchange for sympathy cards, although adding a personal note shows that the card meant something to you. Preworded acknowledgment cards are also acceptable—preferably with a personal note—in cases where hundreds of acknowledgments must be sent.

October 25, 1964

Dear Betty:

I want you to know how much I appreciated your lovely letter of condolence and love—

Having worked with Harpo for forty years, which is much longer than most marriages last, his death left quite a void in my life.

He was worth all the wonderful adjectives that were used to describe him.

He was a nice man in the fullest sense of the word. He loved life and lived it joyously and deeply and that's about as good an epitaph as anyone can have.

My best to your family and my love to you.

Groucho

P.S. This is a hell of a handwriting for a man who is old enough to be your father. I'm sure Melinda's cat could have done as well, but he wouldn't love you as much as I do.

Groucho Marx, a very funny man, had no trouble expressing his deepest feelings to good friends.

Business Occasions

While most people don't associate business with thank-you-note writing, most successful businesses know that expressing appreciation in writing builds morale within the organization and goodwill beyond its doors.

Following business-related events
If you are treated to a business-related meal or other event, it is not necessary to send a thank-you note. For example, if you are the dinner guest of a company who provides services to your organization, a verbal thank-you is sufficient. The same is true for more elaborate events, such as a golfing weekend. On the other hand, sending a note is not incorrect. Just don't overdo it. If a client sends you a gift in appreciation for the work you've done, do send a thank-you note. It lets the client know the gift arrived safely and it demonstrates your good manners.

To show appreciation to employees and business associates
It's always a good idea to write thank-you notes to associates who provide special favors or services, such as a job lead or help on a tough project. If you are an

January 9, 1934

    CAST THIS IS TO THANK ALL OF YOU
FOR YOUR SPLENDID WORK FOR WHICH I
SHALL NEVER CEASE TO BE GRATEFUL
STOP DONT LET THE BAD NEWSPAPER
REVIEWS BOTHER YOU STOP YOU KNOW I
TOLD YOU TO DISCOUNT THEM IN ADVANCE
STOP THIS PLAY WAS NOT WRITTEN FOR
THAT TYPE OF MIND BUT I KNOW YOU WILL
FIND HERE AS IN BOSTON A STEADILY
GROWING AUDIENCE OF THE INTELLIGENT
AND UNPREJUDICED WHO WILL KNOW
WHAT THE PLAY IS ABOUT AND APPRECI-
ATE YOUR GRAND WORK IN MAKING IT
LIVE STOP THIS IS A PLAY WE CAN CARRY
OVER THE CRITICS HEADS STOP SO CARRY
ON WITH CONFIDENCE IN THE FINAL
RESULT AND MAKE THEM LIKE IT STOP
ARE WE DOWNHEARTED NO WE WILL GET
THEM IN THE END STOP AGAIN MY GRATI-
TUDE TO YOU ALL = EUGENE ONEILL

*Eugene O'Neill sent this telegram to the company of
his controversial play* Days Without End.

employer or supervisor, you should send thank-you notes to employees who have made valuable suggestions or outstanding efforts. Such tangible expression of gratitude not only makes employees feel appreciated and boosts their morale, it also helps polish your image.

To show appreciation to customers and suppliers

A note of appreciation to those who have purchased a product or service from you is good business. In particular, thank customers for their first order and also for especially large orders. Thank them, too, for longtime support and for showing courtesies to your sales representatives. You can also help build goodwill by sending notes of appreciation to suppliers—a group that may be as important to your business as loyal customers.

Following a business referral

Jeffrey Dobkin, writing in the *American Salesman*, calls the thank-you letter "the most valuable letter you can write." In this case, he is speaking mostly about expressing thanks for a business referral. The referral, he believes, demonstrates the client's or friend's trust in you and should thus be rewarded. Moreover, by demonstrating your thoughtfulness and attention to detail, the recipient's good opinion of you is reinforced. Your thank-you letter not only expresses your appreciation but also is likely to sit on the recipient's desk for a while or even get passed around. "Without a doubt, this letter is the least costly and most effective piece of advertising I can write, bar none," says Dobkin.

To speakers and volunteers

Those who have served as speakers, such as after-dinner and keynote speakers, deserve a note of appreciation—even if you were dissatisfied with the speech. In cases where the speaker receives an honorarium, include a note with the check.

You should always send a thank-you to everyone who volunteered on behalf of an organization. If you are the leader of the organization or of a department within an organization, be sure to thank everyone who works without pay. Your note of appreciation is the volunteer's only tangible proof that your organization values his or her efforts.

Following a job interview

As a matter of courtesy, you should always write a thank-you letter following a job interview, even if you're not particularly interested in the position. If you want the job, the letter can serve to put your name

Engine Company 211
Brooklyn, NY 11211

To: Community Bookstore Volunteers
Date: Sept. 19, 2001
Subject: Meals

Thank You!! Thank You!! Thank You!!

The officers and members of Hooper Street sincerely appreciate the extraordinary effort your crew has been providing us throughout this horrific ordeal. In the early days of this tragedy, meal preparation was not in the foremost of our minds. As this firehouse had been a staging area for the entire division, the task of feeding hundreds of firefighters was indeed quite formidable. Your group stepped in and assisted. I'm still not quite sure how you got involved. But you did!

You did indeed!

Procedures have changed since those early days and the need for prepared meals is not as necessary as it had been. In an effort to return to some type of normalcy, we will try to procure and prepare our own meals. To that end, it would be a decision by the officer on duty, based on workload and unit availability. There will however be

Occasions and Opportunities: When to Send Thank-You Notes

occasions when we may be unable to complete
that task.

It would be assuring to know that in isolated
cases we would still be able to call on you
for relief.

> With Greatest Appreciation,
> Lt. John F. Shoemaker
> Eng. 211 Group 9

*Notice the date on this memo. If Lt. Shoemaker could
find the time to write a thank-you note, anybody could.*

45

before the potential employer again. Moreover, because the letter gives you an opportunity to add a forgotten qualification or emphasize your fitness for the job, it can reinforce your position as an applicant.

3

Appearances and Impressions: What Form and Paper to Use

orm and paper matter—but not that much. What matters most is that you let your gratitude be known. A note written on a Big Chief tablet with a number-two pencil is better than nothing. However, some forms are better than others from the recipient's standpoint—and that's what counts. As a rule, you want the effort (yours) to match the gift/kindness/service (theirs). This usually means expressing your heartfelt thanks by writing a note, putting it in an envelope, and sending it by mail. If you're a member of—or aspire to—the social elite, your note cards will be made of heavy paper and bear an engraved monogram or name; otherwise, any note cards will do.

Occasionally, typewritten letters are preferable to handwritten notes; sometimes an e-mailed thank-you is acceptable; on rare occasions a faxed note will do; even a preprinted note can be OK. All, of course, are always better than nothing. Following is a hierarchy of note-writing forms, listed roughly in order of most to least "correct." (For a quick reference, see the table in the appendix.)

Handwritten on social stationery or correspondence cards

If it's important for you to be very correct, you'll write your notes on what is called "social stationery" or

"correspondence cards" (also known as "informals").
Social stationery is good-quality folded notepaper,
ivory or white, that includes a name or monogram on
the front. (Amy Vanderbilt says you should never use
notepaper that says "thank you" on the top fold.)
Informals or correspondence cards, which have no
fold, are made from three-ply stock, either white or
ecru, and measure 6¾ by 4¼ inches. Your name is
printed across the top, and your address is printed in
two lines on the back flap of the envelope. You can
have your name or monogram either engraved or
thermographed ("raised printing," a process that gives
the lettering an engraved appearance and is less
expensive). Offset printing is less expensive than
either engraving or thermography but does not look as
elegant as the other methods.

If you're using social stationery or correspondence
cards to acknowledge wedding gifts, the imprinted
name can be the writer's only, or, if sent after the wedding, it can be the married couple's names (Mr. and
Mrs. Ernest Bellweather, or Penelope and Ernest
Bellweather, or, on separate lines, Penelope Louise
Fitzgerald / Ernest Bradford Bellweather). Or you can
imprint just the first names of the bride and groom
(Penelope and Ernest), a style that allows you to use
the note cards both before and after the wedding. If you

choose a monogram and you're a man, a not-yet-married woman, or a woman who will be retaining her maiden name, the monogram should consist of the initials of your first, middle, and last or maiden names. If you're married and taking your husband's last name, the monogram should consist of your first name, maiden name, and married surname.

Of course, you'll write your notes by hand, using either blue or black ink. (Some say it must be black.) Experts advise using cursive writing, not printing, unless your handwriting is illegible. (I always print because I've forgotten how to write in cursive; I can't imagine anyone I know caring.) Some experts also advise that you begin your note on the bottom half of the note card (if you're using the folded variety). Follow this advice if you want to be conventionally correct; otherwise, if you want to use the whole page to show your appreciation, go ahead. The recipient will like it.

Social stationery, correspondence cards, or plain white paper are the classic forms for wedding gifts. However, you need not adhere to these standards. Some wedding-etiquette experts suggest using social stationery or correspondence cards for formal weddings, but for informal weddings, use other styles of note cards—even those printed with "thank you" on the top fold. The trick, of course, is to determine whether your wedding qualifies as formal or informal.

Handwritten on "ordinary" note cards or paper

Some people use social stationery (described above) for formal occasions, such as weddings or funerals, but use less formal stationery or cards for all other occasions. Most of us use decorated note cards—the kind you buy in boxed sets—for thank-you notes. Notepaper, decorated or not, is also a good choice. Of course, you'll write these notes by hand. Even some business occasions call for handwritten notes, such as thanking your boss for going to bat for you or thanking your host for a business-related golf outing.

Typewritten on stationery

A formal thank-you letter—one that looks like a business letter—is sometimes preferable to a handwritten note. As a rule, you should use this format for acknowledging exceptional service, kindness, or helpfulness by a business or governmental employee. Because such letters invariably wind up in someone's file, type the letter in standard business format, using 8½-by-11-paper.

You can also consider a typewritten letter to acknowledge a job well done. Provided the letter is clearly not boilerplate, typewritten business-style letters lend a certain air of authority. I would rather receive from my boss a well-written job-well-done letter typewritten on the company letterhead than one written by hand. It looks more serious and "official."

For other occasions, stick with the handwritten notes (unless your handwriting is illegible). Handwritten notes are generally considered warmer and more personal, and they avoid raising suspicions that you're using a template. Nevertheless, I have received, from dear friends, word-processed thank-you letters that are gems. (Two of them are included in this book.) A word processor allows you to edit and rewrite until you convey the message just the way you want it, thus communicating more care and thoughtfulness than even a handwritten note. If you're a stickler for creating handwritten notes for all social occasions but want to take special care with the spelling and composition, consider using the computer to compose and spell-check the perfect note, and then copy it by hand. Your decision regarding whether or not to create a typewritten note may depend on the recipient—some will care, others will not. Use your judgment.

E-mail messages

As a rule, I don't recommend sending e-mailed thank-you notes. In my opinion, an e-mailed note is too slap-dash. It lacks class, warmth, and generosity. It indicates that even though your impulse is to express your gratitude, you don't want to make much of an effort to do so. The recipient—however subliminally—is aware of this. The effort you make to create a thank-you note should be roughly commensurate with the effort or generosity of the person to whom you owe thanks.

That said, e-mailed thanks are sometimes acceptable and certainly are better than nothing. You might, for example, use e-mail to thank a business associate for helping you on a project or to thank a close friend for an informal dinner. Certainly, if you'd be unlikely to otherwise express your gratitude, send the e-mail. When you do, craft it as though you were writing a note by hand. Use a salutation, take care with the message (and spelling), and include a complimentary close, such as "sincerely" or "love."

David Clark Scott, writing in *The Christian Science Monitor*, reports that e-mailed notes of thanks are on the rise, even though "etiquette mavens eschew it." He especially values this form after the Christmas holidays when the college-bowl games take up his spare time. He suggests writing e-mail notes during a lunch break at work. (Of course, you can also create hand-written notes on your lunch break—or during television commercials, for that matter.) If e-mailed notes are the accepted form for expressing gratitude among your pals, go ahead, although in this electronic age, the increasingly rare handwritten note arriving in a real mailbox is sure to elicit greater pleasure than one composed of bits and bytes.

At any rate, don't even think of using e-mail to thank people for wedding gifts. And don't send an e-mail message to express gratitude for especially generous gifts or for overnight or longer stays as a guest in someone's home. (Overnight stays with relatives may be an exception.) Also never use e-mail for letters destined for someone's personnel file or for an important business thank-you, such as for a job interview.

Electronic cards

Electronic cards are those you can get and send on the Internet from sites such as *e-cards.com* and *bluemountain.com*. They are classed as a "social expression product," of all things. As a rule, avoid sending such "cards" to express your gratitude. These cards cost nothing, or next to nothing; the thought and effort are minimal. Thank-you notes are gifts, after all, and the e-card is a cheap one. The recipient of the note knows this.

As is often true, there are exceptions to this rule and occasions when an e-card may be OK and even appropriate. For example, my husband received an e-card from a young friend (an eighteen-year-old) who was expressing his appreciation for the gift of hard-to-get tickets to view the stars through the telescope at a university observatory. The young man had already thanked my husband by phone. The e-card was a follow-up note of gratitude after the event. (E-cards let you write your own sentiment, if you choose.) In this case, the choice was just right; it indicated the young man's thoughtfulness, expressed his gratitude, and provided a report on how things went. What's more, an e-card seemed perfectly suited to this person, who has for years communicated electronically with my husband. Far from being insulted by the "gift," my husband was quite pleased. In most cases, however, recipients of your thanks will be much more pleased by a handwritten note.

If you're thinking about sending an e-thank-you-card, consider the feelings of the recipient. An e-card—with your own message—might be fine to send to certain people under certain circumstances, but in most cases, resist this cheap and easy solution. And certainly, never use an e-card to thank someone for a wedding gift or other "serious" gift or for a particularly generous act of kindness.

Faxed messages

A faxed message is better than nothing, but it doesn't speak particularly well of you. For one thing, the recipient is paying for the fax paper as well as for the time the letter occupies the machine. Besides, you've already taken the time to write the note. You might as well take another minute or two to put the message in an envelope. A faxed message is acceptable only if the recipient lives in a remote place, doesn't have e-mail, and the postal service is iffy—in other words, virtually never.

Preprinted cards

Preprinted cards fall into two categories: "custom-made" cards engraved with a sentiment of gratitude, and commercial cards bearing a sentiment written by an employee of the card company. The engraved style is appropriate for a public official who wants to acknowledge an overwhelming number of congratulatory

Thank you so much for your kind gift. I appreciate your thoughtfulness and generosity. You have my best wishes.

Bill Clinton

Here's an example of a preprinted card from a public official. It was printed on a plain white card with the presidential seal.

messages received from strangers after winning an election or receiving some other honor.

A commercial card that exactly expresses your feelings may be acceptable if you also include a handwritten message. However, because your personal message is infinitely more valuable to the recipient than the preprinted message, you'd be better off writing your own sentiments on plain paper. Never use preprinted cards to express thanks for wedding gifts.

The bottom line

One person may be insulted at receiving an e-mailed note of thanks for hosting you for a weekend; another might not care; another may be pleased. Thank-you notes written on expensive, engraved correspondence cards might impress or gratify some people; others might view it as odd; some might think you're overreaching your station. In choosing which form and paper to use, the most important considerations are the feelings and sensibilities of the recipient. At the same time, your choice should reflect the occasion, your relationship to the recipient, and your character.

As the following excerpt from a "Mail Call" article in *The New York Times* explains, both your choice of form and paper and your handwriting communicate their own messages:

This is what happens when you send electronic mail, as millions of Americans now do. Your fingers fly; so, in a sense, do your words; and you never run out of stamps. But if you're the recipient and the correspondence is personal, you are not getting all the message. True, you're getting some of it, the part that is articulated anyway. The rest, however, is in the handwriting, and in whether it is slanting up or down, backward or forward. It is in the loop—or dangling tail—of the "y," and the size of the caps and the spaces between the letters. It is in whether the writing is Palmer Method (the correspondent is getting on), clerk's cursive (he took a course) or illegible (he is either un- or over-educated).

It is in the paper, too. Was it torn from a legal pad or a child's lined notebook? Was it lifted from a hotel? Does it have flowers on it? Is it monogrammed? Is there a name and address printed at the top? Or—we're talking money or the pretense thereto—a name and address engraved at the top? Is it flimsy? Weighty? Watermarked? Adorably pink? Cerebrally gray? Chastely white? Are there traces of tears? Or ketchup? Or perfume? Yes, you can print out your E-mail. You can even tie it with a ribbon and cache it in your desk. But on the nights when you want to revisit your old friends, enemies, husbands, wives, lovers, parents, and siblings—and open the drawer to retrieve them— they won't be there. Not entirely.

To have them you need everything that went into their letters. That was a lot more than words.

The other day, I wrote to a friend using a note card I had bought especially for her. As I wrote, I began to become impatient with the slow, laborious process of writing by hand, scratching my pen across the rough surface of the paper. How much easier and quicker to dash off a quick e-mail message—and how tempting! Indeed. But what was the hurry? Using a computer, I might gain a minute or two. And what would my friend—who has been deciphering my miserable handwriting for more than forty years—have received from me? Only the words.

4

Writing and Composing I: How to Craft the Social Thank-You Note

A friend of mine, having been invited to the wedding of her neighbor's son, drove twenty miles to a store where the wedding couple was registered and purchased pieces of the desired china, spending considerably more than was her habit for wedding gifts. The wedding was in August. In December, she received a nearly illegible note with no salutation: "Thank you for the wedding gift. It was nice that you could join us." Such a meager expression of gratitude simply won't do. The note was too late, too impersonal, too short, and too generic. It did not come close to showing the appreciation my friend deserved for her time, money, and effort. I suspect the couple sat down and wrote this same message on a big stack of cards, assembly-line fashion, and then stuffed them in envelopes and addressed them. And for this, it took more than three months to respond!

You can do better. Here are some general rules for writing thank-you notes as well as guidelines and examples for writing specific types of notes, such as acknowledgment of weddings gifts.

Thanks for gifts

A note of thanks can be as short as three sentences, provided you say something about the qualities of the gift and express your appreciation. Make an effort to sound enthusiastic. Even if you don't especially like the gift, do convey your appreciation for the thought and effort that someone has spent on your behalf. ("It was so thoughtful of you to remember our anniversary with that one-of-a-kind chip-and-dip set.")

When composing the note, be yourself. Avoid using words or phrases you wouldn't ordinarily use. For example, I wouldn't say, "The cut-glass pitcher is perfectly marvelous!" This just doesn't sound like me. However, you will likely use a slightly different style and tone in a letter to a close friend than to someone with whom your relationship is more distant or formal. ("The electronic organizer is amazing! I've been hankering for one of these for years," versus, "The electronic organizer will be a big help in my new position. I deeply appreciate your thoughtfulness in selecting such a useful gift.")

At a minimum, a thank-you note for a gift should include these elements:

> 🌑 *Reference to the present itself.* Mention the specific item you received. ("Thank you for the magnificent collectors' edition of *War and Peace.*") Never refer to the item you received by the general term "gift" or "present," as in "Thank you for

27 December 56

I have been highly enjoying the beautiful book
[*Three Mystics*] about St. Theresa and St. John and
El Greco and so for that matter has my mother.
And we christened the water pitcher last Sunday
and she proclaimed it was just suited to her needs
and was highly gratified that the spout didn't drip.
So we are both most grateful. Me I am glad that at
least half the holidays are over and I hope we soon
get rid of the fruit cake and turkey. We had our
Christmas dinner on Sunday and for Christmas
I demanded and got meatballs and turnip greens.

This thank-you for Christmas gifts is from author
Flannery O'Connor to William Sessions.

the lovely gift." The giver will infer that you don't remember what was given. Besides, this form of expression indicates your laziness and lack of consideration for the feelings of the giver, and it does not adequately express gratitude for someone else's generosity.

🐾 *Detailed remarks about its qualities*. Say something specific about the attributes, craftsmanship, or other qualities of the gift. ("The workmanship on the beautiful hand-tooled leather binding is exquisite.")

🐾 *Reasons why you like it*. State what you like about the gift and how you are going to use it. ("I've been looking for just this edition to add to my collection. Of course, I'm also looking forward to reading it—something I've been meaning to do for years.")

🐾 *A closing sentence*. The closing sentence can be a final thank-you or expression of appreciation, or it can be unrelated to the gift, such as greetings to family members, an expression of your affection, or an indication of the ways in which your relationship to the giver is special. ("It's been such a blessing for me to have you for a godfather.")

September 17, 1954

Dear Phyllis:

This book inscribed
from Phyllis McGinley
Is more precious to me
Than a bust of McKinley.

Many thanks,
Groucho

This thank-you poem made me laugh out loud.

Here's an example of a five-sentence note:

Dear Susan,

I love the sweater you sent for my birthday. It's a gorgeous shade of red, and will be perfect with the new slacks I just ordered. I'm planning on wearing it to the Stanford/Cal game this Saturday. Many thanks!

I hope we can find a time to get together this fall. It's been too long!

Love,

Marge

This one is only three sentences:

Dear Bob and Sue,

Thank you so much for the gorgeous Italian hand-painted serving platter. It's such a showpiece that Mary and I can't decide whether to hang it on the wall or use it for meals—we'll probably do both!

You'll be among our first dinner guests after we return from our honeymoon.

Fondly,

Fritz

January 9, 1922

Mr. L. Robinson

I wish to express through you to each member of the Senior class my deep appreciation for the fountain pen you so kindly and thoughtfully gave me Christmas.

This gift, like all the others, is characterized by simplicity and thoughtfulness, which I hope each member will make the slogan of their lives.

As your father, it is needless for me to keep saying, I hope, except for emphasis, that each one of my children will rise to the full height of your possibilities, which means the possession of these eight cardinal virtues which constitutes a lady or a gentleman.

1st. Be clean both inside and outside.

2nd. Who neither looks up to the rich or down on the poor.

3rd. Who loses, if needs be, without squealing.

4th. Who wins without bragging.

5th. Who is always considerate of women, children, and old people.

6th. Who is too brave to lie.

7th. Who is too generous to cheat.

8th. Who takes his share of the world and lets other people have theirs.

May God help you carry out these eight cardinal virtues and peace and prosperity by yours through life.

Lovingly yours,
G. W. Carver

George Washington Carver sent this thank-you note to the members of his senior class at the Tuskegee Institute, where he was head of the agriculture department.

Here's a thank-you for an especially generous wedding gift:

Dear Mr. and Mrs. Wentworth,

We were thrilled to receive an entire place setting of our silver from you. Such a generous gift! We enjoy hosting dinner parties, especially when we can set the table with beautiful silver. Your gift brings us closer to that possibility. Thank you!

It was wonderful to see you at the wedding. Your presence helped make our day special.

Sincerely,
Penny Fox and Paul Stuart

Of course, when you're writing to a friend and just being yourself, your notes will be more interesting than the above made-up examples. Consider this note written by Eugene O'Neill to a friend, Carl Van Vechten:

Dear Carl:

The records arrived—and they are some camelias! As you expected the "Saint James Infirmary" is right in my alley! I am memorizing the words. Do you know [jazz trumpeter] Mr. [Louis] Armstrong? If so, give him my fraternal benediction. He is a darb.

*"Empty Bed" is grand—also my old favorites
"Soft Pedal" & "Sing Sing" that Paul Robeson
introduced me to.*

*Many, many thanks! It is good to have [jazz
singer] Bessie [Smith] around wahooing in the
peaceful French evenings. She makes the ancestral
portraits of the provincial noblesse shudder—or
maybe it's shimmy!*

Carlotta joins me in all best to Fania & you.

*I'm hard at work. Are you? How is N.Y. these
days? I see I've joined the Banned-In-Boston club
of which I believe you're a member. Wa-hoo!*

Gene O'Neill

Special situations

Occasionally, acknowledging gifts—especially wedding gifts—can be tricky, as when you receive

🖋 *Gifts of money*. Express gratitude for monetary
gifts by mentioning how you will use the money.
("I'll put the check toward the car I'm hoping to
buy.") Some experts advise against mentioning
the amount of the gift; others think it's a good
idea. Use your own judgment. If you don't mention the amount, describe it as "generous."

🍃 *Unidentifiable gifts.* If you can't figure out how a gift is to be used, do your best to describe it and show your appreciation. ("The engraved silver piece you sent has generated lots of comments around here. Such a generous gift!")

🍃 *Gifts that are not to your taste.* If you don't like the gift, you can show your appreciation by focusing on the kindness of the giver instead of on the gift. You can avoid lying by mentioning truthful qualities of the gift. ("Thank you so much for the colorful lap blanket. It simply exudes warmth.")

🍃 *Duplicate gifts.* If the gift is a duplicate or if there is a problem with it, don't mention it. Don't ask where the gift was purchased so that you can return it. If you exchange a gift, don't inform the giver. Conveying your disappointment to the giver, who has been generous on your behalf, is unkind.

🍃 *A gift that arrives broken.* If you receive a broken gift, don't inform the sender. Instead, write your thank-you note as if all were well. That way, you'll avoid worrying or disappointing the sender. If the gift was sent from a store, try contacting them to see if you can obtain a replacement. If that doesn't work, forget it.

🍃 *Gifts from multiple givers.* If you receive a single gift from more than one person (unless it's a family), thank each individual—and don't send identical notes to each. The editors of *Bride's* magazine suggest the following rule: If you receive a single gift from several relatives or friends, write each a separate note, provided the group numbers less than ten. If the group numbers more than ten, one thank-you note is sufficient, "but be sure to thank everyone in person as well," they advise. I'm not sure I agree. Ten notes don't strike me as too burdensome. On the other hand, in certain situations, a single thank-you is sufficient. For example, if you've received a gift from a large number of people—say from the 150 people who work at your firm, many of whom you don't know—write a thank-you letter to the office manager asking her to convey your appreciation and gratitude on your behalf.

When to mail your notes

Write and mail your notes as soon as possible. Most etiquette experts allow two weeks to mail thank-you notes for gifts other than wedding gifts. Of course, earlier is better. Try to get the note in the mail within a day or two of receiving the gift.

March 2, 1918

Dear Mither,

The box came tonight and we just opened it at the Press room the cake sure was great. There were about four of the fellows here and we opened the box and ate the cake. It was a peach, I am going to take the rest of the grub home and Carl and I will finish it up. The fellows all agreed that Mother Hemingstein must be some cook. Your praises were sung in loud and stentorian tones. The cake sure fed a multitude of starving and broke newspaper men tonight....

> Good Luck
> Ernie
> Love to everyone
> Ernie

At age nineteen, Ernest Hemingway was a cub reporter at the Kansas City Star. *This thank-you letter to his mother is the first I've seen with two closings and two signatures.*

Acknowledging wedding gifts is a different matter, especially now that so many people bring gifts to the wedding rather than sending them to the bride and/or groom prior to the wedding. (The latter is a more thoughtful practice, because it saves the bridal party from hauling the gifts from the wedding site to their final destination.)

If you've waited too long

If you've put off note writing for an embarrassingly long time, go ahead and write tardy notes, but now each note must be long and effusive—and without excuses. Another strategy for too-late notes is to write a letter saying how much you've been enjoying the gift, using words implying that this is a follow-up to your original thank-you note, which of course never existed. But I disapprove of this ploy because it's not truthful and because, for the recipient, it casts doubt on his or her memory or on the reliability of the post office.

In a *Town and Country* magazine article, Catherine Calvert describes the results of her lapsed note writing:

I remember bogging down while working my way through a very long list of wedding-present thank-yous. The first few were buoyed by the joy of using stationery with my new initials, the next hundred a connect-the-dots exercise in getting the job done. But almost at the end, I petered out. It took a call from *Tiffany & Co.*, gently inquiring whether I'd actually received the five china plates because the donor was concerned, to send me back to my desk. There I concocted an abject apology and fulsome thanks, after rejecting all sorts of alternatives, like moving overseas. I winced for months whenever I encountered that woman of a certain age, gracious to her gloved fingertips, who'd seen my seamy, sloppy side.

Protocol for wedding-gift thank-yous

Acknowledging wedding gifts often raises protocol questions, such as

- 💬 *When to mail the notes*. Etiquette experts have varying notions about acceptable time limits for sending thank-yous following the receipt of wedding gifts, ranging from two weeks to three months. I think two or three months is too long to keep gift-givers waiting to hear from you. Shoot for two weeks after the wedding or honeymoon.
- 💬 *Salutations to use*. Use the gift-givers' first names ("Dear Sarah and Jim") in the salutation unless

you don't know them well or your relationship is a formal one, in which case you should write the formal name ("Dear Mr. and Mrs. Wentworth" or "Dear Mr. Higgenbottom and Ms. Wentworth"). If the gift-giver has a professional title, a formal salutation should include that title ("Dear Dr. and Ms. Johnston" or "Dear Drs. Livingston"). If you are writing the note to someone who is close to your spouse but not to you, use the term he or she uses ("Dear Uncle Ed and Aunt Bea").

- *How to close.* Choose a complimentary close that reflects your relationship to the giver. You can choose among "sincerely," "affectionately," "fondly," "love," "cordially," and so forth.

- *Signing the note.* The writer of the note should sign it. In this case, you should mention your spouse in the body of the note. ("Mary and I deeply appreciate the generous check you sent.") For your signature, use your full name for people who don't know you well; otherwise sign just your first name.

- *Acknowledging acknowledgments from registries.* Some bridal registries notify the recipient when a gift is on its way. Such notifications, which indicate a delay in shipment, usually include the names of the givers as well as a description of the gift. Rather than allow the givers to wonder why they have not received your thanks, write a brief note to inform them of the situation. ("We just received word from Tiffany's that the silver candlesticks you so thoughtfully selected for George and me will be arriving within two weeks. We're looking forward to their arrival and will write again soon.")

🖎 *Acknowledging those who helped.* You should send a thank-you note to everyone who helped you with the wedding, such as ushers, bridesmaids, and those who hosted parties for you.

See chapter 6, "Discipline and Organization: How to Tackle Big Jobs," for more tips on dealing with wedding-gift thank-yous.

Thanks for overnight stays, parties, and dinners

Whether your hosts entertained you for a week at their summer cabin or let you crash on their foldout couch for a weekend, they deserve a note of thanks. Bringing a bottle of wine, a box of chocolates, or a bouquet of flowers does not absolve you of your note-writing duty. You still need to show your appreciation by writing a note of gratitude for the time, work, and money your hosts spent on your behalf.

Dear Connie and Speed,

Thank you for all the scissors—we love them!
The pruning shears are perfect because I love
bringing home fresh flowers and our yard is now
blooming. Matt tried to cut through a penny and it
didn't quite make it, but it may have been Matt
and not the scissors.

We are really looking forward to seeing you at
the wedding, which seems to be approaching
quickly. It is wonderful to have so many family
and friends help us celebrate this exciting time.

Fondly,
Jennifer

*A week after I sent a wedding gift (a collection of
scissors, one of which was touted as being able to cut
through a penny), I received this note from the bride-to-
be, Jennifer Ill (now McKenzie). Not only was the note
sent quickly, but it was also written on the socially correct stationery: good quality white paper, engraved on
the top fold with the bride's maiden name.*

In cases where the hosts are a married couple, some etiquette experts advise you to address your note to the wife (the one traditionally responsible for taking care of guests) but to include the husband in the body of the letter; others advise you to address both wife and husband. Your decision on this may depend on the role each played. Use your own judgment.

Make an effort to send your note of thanks within three to five days of your departure. For dinners or other events, your hosts should receive your note within a day or two.

In general, the length of the letter should reflect the amount of effort expended by your hosts. For example, if you have been wined and dined for several days, your letter should consist of several paragraphs. State what a good time you had, mention something nice about the host's house or its setting, perhaps offer compliments about the food, and discuss specific activities you enjoyed:

Dear Louise and Tom,

George and I had a wonderful time at your home last weekend. You did an amazing job of entertaining us. The accommodations were comfy, the meals fantastic, and the activities memorable.

The view from the guest room is gorgeous. We particularly enjoyed watching the fog drifting in from the ocean. And the flowers you placed in our room made us feel especially welcome.

You've got a real knack for planning just the right mix of activities and relaxation time. We loved bicycling around Golden Gate Park as well as the tour of Alcatraz. I'd never have dreamed a visit to a prison could be so fascinating.

Many, many thanks for seeing to it that we had such a great time. We deeply appreciate your efforts and feel blessed to have such dear friends.

> Love,
> Sally

If your stay was a simple overnight, it can be shorter:

Dear Fred,

Thanks for putting me up for the night. I know it was an imposition, and I appreciate the special effort you made to provide me with all the comforts of home. I'll give you a call as soon as I get home.

> Later,
> Mike

If someone has hosted a party for you, a thank-you note is required:

Dear Geraldine,

Thank you so much for throwing such a wonderful party on my behalf. I enjoyed myself enormously, as I'm sure everyone did. Everything you served was scrumptious. I especially loved the salmon mousse. The table decorations were beautiful. You are a woman of many talents

I know what an effort it is to plan and prepare a sit-down dinner for so many people, and I appreciate it more than I can say.

Fondly,

Laura

Thanks for kindness and service

Sending a note of thanks to people who have been kind or helpful to you or have provided you with good service is an especially thoughtful act. You are not obligated to express your gratitude for these deeds in writing; neither does the recipient expect it. Your note is a gift. It will likely bring happiness to the recipient and will probably also be saved. Particularly worthy of

Dear Mom,

I don't know what I would have done without you. You were (are) positively wonderful—patient, understanding, loving, encouraging. Those first few days—oh, boy I thought I had made the worst decision of all times. Well, thanks to you I'm starting to see some light at the end of the tunnel. At my last P.T. [physical therapy] visit I reached 105° (120° is full flexation) and I may be able to get the immobilizer (sp?) off as early as two weeks away.

Anyway, thanks again. I suppose I am forever indebted to you and you've already cancelled future plans for "the home," figuring "Of course – I'll be at Matt's pad – he and his family will be taking wonderful care of me." Well, that's just fine with me!

Love, Matt

This treasured note is from a young-adult son, Matthew McKenzie, to his mother, thanking her for taking care of him following elective knee surgery and promising, in return, to care for her in her old age.

your thanks are those faceless people who serve you well, such as the woman who cleans your office at night or the man who delivers your newspaper without fail. One woman wrote a thank-you note to the staff at the animal shelter on the first anniversary of the day she adopted her two cats. "I thought about all the abused animals [the staff] saw," she says, and "about the relatively thankless job they face every day, and I wanted to show them my appreciation." Another woman wrote a thank-you note to the person who created a lovely garden in the midst of an "otherwise drab neighborhood."

There is no end to the opportunities for sending such notes, and no "rules" for writing them. Just mention the deed or service and express your gratitude for it. If you're planning to express your appreciation to someone who served you well in the line of duty, such as an airline employee, it's best for the recipient if your letter is a formal one—typed on standard-sized paper—and sent to the employee's boss or to the president of the company. If you don't know these names, you can send the letter in care of the customer-relations department. You can find names and addresses on the Internet, or you can check your phone book or library registries.

Here is an example of a thank-you in response to a kind deed:

Dear Mary,

I want you to know how deeply grateful I am for all your help after I broke my leg—taking me home from the hospital, carting me to and from my doctor appointments, preparing those wonderful casseroles, and just generally looking after me. I don't know what I would have done without you.

I appreciate your kindness more than I can say and hope that I can return the favor some day—without, of course, your having to break *your* leg. Sincere thanks for being such a dear friend.

> Much love,
> Emily

Thanks for funeral-related acts of kindness

If possible, within six weeks of a funeral you should send written thanks to those who helped out with the proceedings, such as pallbearers and speakers, and also to those who sent flowers and letters of condolence. In expressing gratitude for letters of condolence, thank the writer for what he wrote, letting him know you have taken his words to heart. Consider including a funny and warm anecdote about the person whom you are mourning. In this way, you let the recipient of your note know it's OK to speak of the deceased in a similar way. To help people learn how you're getting along, indicate how you're feeling and coping with your loss.

Here are a couple of examples of funeral-related thank-you notes:

Dear Fred,

Your thoughtful letter following the death of my dad meant a lot to me. I especially appreciate your reminiscences about the years the two of you spent together in the Forest Service. Most of those stories were new to me. They help round out my understanding of my father as a young man. I hope you know that my dad thought very highly of you and that he also remembered your years together with fondness.

You were so kind to take the time to share your memories with me. Thank you. It helps.

Sincerely,

Raymond Hauser

Dear Marjorie and Phil,

The spray of yellow roses you sent for Martha's funeral was magnificent. Did you know yellow

roses were her favorite? Thank you for them.
Thank you, too, for your kind attentions. It helps to
have friends like you by my side.

Needless to say, this is a tough time for me.
I miss Martha terribly and am doing my best to
keep on an even keel. The support of friends and
family is a big help.

Gratefully,
John

A final word

As you sit down to craft your thank-you note, bear in
mind that, just as a gift or act of kindness comes from
a spirit of generosity, so too should your expression of
gratitude. French philosopher Andrè Comte-Sponville,
who has made a study of virtue, says, "Generosity ele-
vates us *toward others*, as it were, and toward ourselves
as beings freed from the pettiness that is the self."
More than that, he adds, "accompanied by gentleness,
it is called kindness."

5

Writing and Composing II: How to Craft the Business Thank-You Note

It may be that, in the business world, the practice of writing thank-you notes is on the rise. I have only anecdotal evidence to support this claim, but I think research would bear it out. In the space of one week I received two *handwritten* business-related thank-you notes. One, written on quality paper with the store's name embossed on the front, came from the person who took my phone order for a pair of shoes. The note said, "It was my pleasure helping you place your order today. I hope you will be very pleased with those gray shoes. Thanks again for shopping with Nordstrom.com." The second—also written on quality notepaper—was from the young man who fixed my computer. It was a complicated job and he worked most of the day, so I served him lunch. His note thanked me for my hospitality. My husband and I have both received thank-you notes following the purchase of a car, a practice that seems to have become commonplace.

Evidently, in the moneymaking realm, people have discovered that it pays to write thank-you notes. In fact, at an important management conference on leadership in the twenty-first century, which featured such widely-respected gurus as Peter Drucker and Steven Covey, one of the tips for management success was to write thank-you notes!

Many business occasions call for written expressions of gratitude: a job well done, client and customer referrals, job interviews, recommendations, business-related social events, volunteer work, leads to a potential prospect, a major purchase, charitable contributions, a presentation made to your service club. Writing thank-yous for these occasions speaks well for you and lifts the spirits of those to whom you express your appreciation. It's also good business.

How business notes are different from social notes

Writing a business-related thank-you note is not much different from writing a social note. Either way, it's a personal process—one person expressing gratitude to another. In some respects, however, a business thank-you *is* different from a social thank-you. For one thing, more may be at stake. Getting that job may hinge on the quality of the thank-you note following your interview, or repeat sales may result from your thoughtful expression of gratitude. (Remember the chairman of the Detroit Symphony Orchestra; his thank-you note was instrumental in garnering $2.5 million from a generous donor.)

What's more, if you're writing on behalf of your company, you are representing the company just as

Dear Scott,

Thank you so much for your wonderful portrayal of Tec-Ed and how we help improve the usability of high-tech products. You captured the heart of what we do in an interesting, appealing article. Would you also thank Elli Garfinkel for his unique photo?

Your article has made all of us at Tec-Ed even more than usually proud to have our firm's headquarters in Ann Arbor!

Regards,
Stephanie Rosenbaum

P.S. Lily the cat sends a thank-you purr!

This note, written by a company president, expresses appreciation to a journalist for a well-written article.

you would in a face-to-face meeting. (In fact, the letter is a substitute for a face-to-face meeting.) You want your letter to create a favorable impression. You also want to elicit a positive attitude toward you and your company. Every thank-you note builds goodwill for your organization and has the potential for increasing sales. In fact, the thank-you letter, more than any other, may be the most important letter you write for building goodwill. For these reasons, it's worth your time to write a business-related thank-you note with care.

Some tips for writing business thank-yous

Because the stakes may be high and you want to create a good impression, your business-related thank-you letters should be well-crafted. The rewards are worth your time and effort. Here are some tips:

- *Make it personal.* A thank-you note, even one written in a business context, is not sent from one organization to another but from one person to another. Use the pronouns *I* and *you*, just as you would when carrying on a conversation. (You can also use *we* when referring to your organization or team.) Make it clear by the letter contents (not just the address) that you wrote the letter for only the recipient. Avoid form letters.

🖋 *Be yourself.* Your thank-you note should sound like you. It should be conversational and friendly, not stiff and formal. But don't go overboard. Choose your words and phrases carefully. You want your letter to be graceful and polished.

🖋 *Make it lively.* Avoid stodgy clichés, such as "your patronage is appreciated" or "I am in receipt of" or "I wish to state." Instead, use livelier and more personal phrases, such as "our whole team appreciates" or "I was delighted to receive" or "I want you to know."

🖋 *Use correct spelling and grammar.* Use the spelling- and grammar-checking features of your word-processing software or use a dictionary if you're unsure about spelling. Or ask a colleague to check your work.

Handwritten versus typed

You can either handwrite or type business-related thank-you notes. Handwritten letters are warmer and more personal; typed letters are more businesslike and look more serious.

5th April, 1951

Dear Miss Hanff:

For nearly two years I have been working as a cataloguer at Marks and Co. and would like to thank you very much for my share-out in the parcels which you've been sending.

I live with my great-aunt who is 75, and I think that if you had seen the look of delight on her face when I brought home the meat and tin of tongue, you would have realized just how grateful we are. It's certainly good to know that someone so many miles away can be so kind and generous to people they haven't even seen, and I think that everyone in the firm feels the same.

If at any time you know of anything that you would like sent over from London, I will be most happy to see to it for you.

Sincerely,
Bill Humphries

The book Eighty-Four Charing Cross Road *is a collection of letters exchanged between Helene Hanff, of New York City, and the employees of Marks and Company, a London-based dealer in out-of-print books.*

The case for handwritten business thank-yous

Handwritten notes are appropriate for the social side of business, such as thanking the sponsors of a golf outing, or for special kindnesses. For example, you might send a handwritten thank-you note to your boss for seeing to it that you received stock options. Handwritten notes are more impressive than typewritten notes for thanking customers who purchase items from retail businesses. The customer who receives a handwritten note feels acknowledged, special, and appreciated—and likely to give you repeat business. Sending a handwritten note also makes you memorable and sets you apart from your competitors. As Eileen O. Brownell writes in *American Salesman*, the handwritten thank-you note "may truly be the one extraordinary customer service step that brings the client back again and again." If your organization has many customers or clients, you can ask each salesperson or order taker to be responsible for the notes, as was the case for the note I got from Nordstrom.

Augustine Hilton, CEO of Global Management Systems, sends handwritten thank-you cards—mentioning specific accomplishments—to employees' homes. Mailing the cards to the homes, he says, gives employees "an extra-personal stroke when they open the cards surrounded by their family members." His

December 12, 1952

To "her friends at 84, Charing Cross Road":
   The Book-Lovers' Anthology stepped out of its wrappings, all gold-embossed leather and gold-tipped pages, easily the most beautiful book I own including the Newman first edition. It looks too new and pristine ever to have been read by anyone else, but it has been: it keeps falling open at the most delightful places as the ghost of its former owner points me to things I've never read before. Like Tristram Shandy's description of his father's remarkable library which "contained every book and treatise which had ever been wrote upon the subject of great noses." (Frank! Go find me *Tristram Shandy*!)
   I do think it's a very uneven exchange of Christmas presents. You'll eat yours up in a week and have nothing left to show for it by New Year's Day. I'll have mine till the day I die—and die happy in the knowledge that I'm leaving it behind for someone else to love. I shall sprinkle pale pencil marks through it pointing out the best passages to some booklover yet unborn.

   Thank you all. Happy New Year.
                   Helene

This letter was written by Helene Hanff to the employees of Marks and Company.

practice of sending notes to thank employees is part of a larger effort to cultivate an "attitude of gratitude" at his company.

You can use any (tasteful) type of stationery for handwritten notes. If you represent the company, you can use the company letterhead, but the paper should be the smaller-sized note paper (5½ by 8½ inches). If you want to be particularly classy, use correspondence cards—the formal type of card discussed in chapter 3. Marjabelle Young Stewart reports that CEOs especially love to get notes on correspondence cards. "I've heard several of them say that they hired or promoted someone because of it," she says.

The case for typewritten business thank-yous

Send a typewritten thank-you when you want a formal, businesslike look. Typewritten thank-yous are especially appropriate for business-to-business communications, such as for thanking a business owner who has purchased products from your manufacturing company. I have always typed my job-interview thank-yous, but some etiquette experts advise writing these letters by hand on good-quality note paper. Either is acceptable. On the one hand, a typewritten note is easier to read and, if written on business-size paper, fits neatly into a standard file folder; on the other hand, the more personal handwritten note is standard form for most types of thank-yous.

For thanking employees for good work or exceptional service, I recommend a typewritten letter, using an 8½-by-11 business letterhead. As a recipient, I prefer this more formal look. Typewritten letters on a business letterhead seem to hold more authority. Furthermore, such letters are likely to go into personnel files, which are best suited to the standard paper size.

The business-style format

For business-style typewritten thank-you letters, you can use any of the standard business formats:

- *Blocked style*. Date and complimentary close beginning in the middle of the page; each paragraph indented five spaces.
- *Semi-blocked style*. Date and complimentary close beginning in the middle of the page; first line of paragraphs not indented.
- *Full-blocked style*. Everything (date, address, complimentary close) flush with the left margin.

In all of these styles, paragraphs are separated by a double space; the body is single-spaced. Allow two spaces between the last line of the letter and the complimentary close; allow four spaces between the complimentary close and the typed name where the letter will be signed.

Note that if you are using plain paper—not a business letterhead—your address and the date should go in the upper right corner.

The example following shows the full-blocked style— the most commonly used format in the business world.

June 11, 2002

Susan Greensmith, Maintenance Manager
Plymouth Hotels
411 Fog Cutter Avenue
San Francisco, California 91234

Dear Ms. Greensmith,

Thank you for choosing Good Greens to supply and maintain the indoor plants for your Bay Area hotels. I know that creating an attractive and welcoming environment for your guests is a top priority for you, and I want you to know that you can count on Good Greens to help you achieve your goals. Our well-trained staff of designers and horticulturists will see to it that the choice and placement of plants suits the décor and ambience of each hotel; our maintenance crew will keep your plants in optimum health.

Because Good Greens has an excellent customer-satisfaction track record, I'm confident that you'll find our services to your liking. If you have any questions or concerns, give me a call. I sincerely appreciate your business and am looking forward to a successful working relationship with you.

Cordially,

Charles Beckwith
Director of Sales

Salutations and closings

For your salutations, you can use either first or last names, depending on your relationship to the recipient. To a close business associate, use the first name ("Dear Charlie"); otherwise use the social title and last name ("Dear Mr. Smith" or "Dear Dr. Hernandez").

Likewise, choose a complimentary close according to your relationship to the recipient. "Sincerely" works for both formal and personal closings; "Cordially," and "Best wishes," are more personal; "Yours truly," and "Respectfully yours," are more formal.

A sampling of business thank-you notes

As with social thank-yous, the occasions for expressing gratitude in the business world are unlimited. Following are examples of occasions for which notes are most commonly sent.

A job interview

Writing a thank-you letter following a job interview gives you a chance to market yourself one more time and make a positive impression on the interviewer. It helps set you apart from all the other candidates and keeps your name in front of the decision-makers. If you want the job, be sure to write a thank-you letter.

Your letter should underscore your enthusiasm for the company and your fitness for the job. Mention what you liked about the interview, the company, and the position. Also take this opportunity to address any issues or questions that you feel you did not fully answer during the interview. Make the note sincere and warm but also businesslike.

While keeping the letter brief, your letter should at minimum include a statement of appreciation for the interview, an expression of interest in the job and company, a brief restatement of your qualifications, and a statement that anticipates the next step in the recruitment process.

Review your letter carefully before sending it to make sure it is error-free. If you were interviewed by several people, send your note to whomever was the primary contact person and decision-maker. If you wish, you can also send a different note to everyone who interviewed you. To remain competitive in our fast-moving business climate, try to mail your letters the day after the interview. Depending on the culture of the company to which you are applying, an e-mailed letter may be the accepted format. Use your judgment to determine how to make the best impression.

Here's an example of a thank-you note for a job interview:

Dear Ms. Weintraub,

Thank you for meeting with me last week to discuss Hi-Tec Ventures and the project manager position. Your description of the company history was fascinating. I was especially impressed with the company's growth and track record as well as its informal yet results-oriented management style.

The project manager's position strikes me as both challenging and exciting—just the sort of qualities I find appealing. My experience in managing projects for Acme Widgets dovetails neatly with Hi-Tec's requirements, and my academic background in organizational development is well suited to the job demands you described. For these reasons, the position feels like a good fit for me.

I enjoyed talking with you and look forward to hearing from you soon.

Sincerely,

Harold Broser

A job well done

Everyone likes to be appreciated, especially after he or she has made an extraordinary effort for the good of the organization—or even only to please the boss. The note can be either handwritten or typewritten. If you're the boss, send a formal thank-you letter on company stationery, mentioning in detail the importance of the employee's contribution. Such a letter underscores your appreciation of the employee's contribution and provides him with a lasting memento of your appreciation—not to mention a big boost to his morale. Here's an example:

Dear Tony,

I want you to know how much I appreciate the fine work you did heading up the developmental effort for the Whizbang project. It's pretty unusual for a project of this magnitude to come in on time and within the budget, but you pulled it off. What's more, you did it with your usual patience and good humor, qualities that kept your team humming along smoothly. Although you made it look easy, I know you put in some long days (and nights!).

In expressing my thanks, I speak for the whole division. We're all more than pleased with the quality of your work. It's people like you that keep Acme at the top of the heap.

Sincerely,
David Crocker

Even a quickly written e-mailed note boosts morale and can inspire increased loyalty, enthusiasm, and productivity:

Jane

Thanks for a masterful job in putting together the presentation for the Acme account. All your

effort paid off. As you've no doubt heard, the
Acme reps were so impressed they selected us on
the spot. We appreciate your dedication to the
project and the long hours you put in to make it a
success. It's great having you on board!

Steve

If you were the recipient of particularly good service, it's thoughtful to send a note of thanks to the boss
of the person who served you well. For example, a
friend of mine received a copy of this memo, which had
been sent by clients to her boss:

Major thanks to you on behalf of your staff
(namely, Kristie) who led an excellent training on
problem-solving around recruitment. In the 2½
hours, staff had developed a commercial, a draft
brochure, and a strategy for recruiting from local
colleges. That kind of outcome doesn't happen by
accident but is a product of a good staff and an
excellent team leader.

The fact that she saved the memo attests to its
importance to her.

Send job-well-done notes immediately after the
work is completed.

A recommendation

Writing a letter of recommendation takes time and effort. A thank-you note shows your appreciation. When you thank someone for writing a recommendation or reference on your behalf, include any news of how you're faring with your application or job search. At the least, you can promise to let the person know the outcome of your endeavors. You can either write the note by hand or use a word processor. Here's an example:

> Dear Dr. Marsh,
>
> Many thanks for writing a recommendation for me to serve as an intern with National Public Radio. I know it takes time and effort to compose such a letter, and I very much appreciate that you have done so for me. As soon as I hear the outcome from NPR, which should be in a couple of weeks, I'll let you know.
>
> > Gratefully,
> > Ruth

Referrals

By thanking those who send business your way, you not only show your appreciation for the trust they have placed in you, you also reinforce their positive attitude toward you. Besides, it's just good business. Not only is the thank-you a form of advertising, it is an inducement for further referrals.

Here's an example of a thanks-for-your-referral letter:

Dear Sam,

Thanks to your kind referral, the Acme Widgets Company called on us yesterday. It looks like we'll be able to meet their expectations, or even exceed them! Our reputation for quality and dependability is important to us, and we constantly strive to improve the way we do business. We genuinely appreciate your business referrals and value our congenial relationship with your company.

Sincerely,
Maynard Baker

Customers and clients

Most of us are accustomed to receiving form letters from businesses thanking us for our patronage. Such letters usually follow large purchases, such as automobiles, although I have also received thank-you letters for small purchases. The problem is, these letters are invariably form letters. While I appreciate the impulse to express appreciation for my patronage, the letters themselves leave me cold. I usually don't read them. On the other hand, if the letter is handwritten or clearly intended just for me, I am impressed.

Here is an example of a letter thanking a customer for his patronage—but one that could be addressed to anyone:

Dear Mr. Lockwood,

Thank you for choosing Acme Widgets. We appreciate your recent order and value your patronage.

Acme is devoted to providing quality products and top-notch service, and we take pride in our stellar record of customer satisfaction. To that end, I invite you to call me with any question or concern you may have regarding the widgets you purchased.

We look forward to serving you in the future.

Sincerely,
Bob Babbitt
General Manager

Better still, create a letter that is truly personal—one that could not suffice for anyone but the recipient. While the above letter is addressed to "Mr. Lockwood," it could have been sent to any Acme customer. If Acme were a manufacturer and received a large order or an order from a new customer, a thank-you letter that is entirely personal not only will impress the recipient but will go a long way toward building goodwill and retaining that customer. Such a letter might be something like this:

Dear Mr. Lockwood,

Steve Prestwick just showed me your order for 1,000 Acme widgets. Thank you! Your stores have an excellent reputation and we're mighty pleased that Acme products will be part of your inventory. I think you, too, will be pleased with your purchase. Acme widgets are the first choice of people who recognize quality. I'm predicting they'll move quickly off the shelves.

Steve will be giving you a call to see if you need help with display and promotion. Incidentally, he saw to it that your order was placed on the truck this afternoon. You should have it the day after tomorrow.

Thanks again for your order. I'm hoping we can continue to supply you with our top-notch line of widgets. Give me a call if there's anything I can do.

Yours truly,
Bob Babbitt
General Manager

Guest speakers

You should send a thank-you note to a guest speaker, even if you're paying her and even if you didn't like her performance. Letters to the not-so-good speaker will be more difficult to write, of course. Don't express your negative feelings and don't feel required to lie. Instead, thank the speaker for taking the time to participate in your program.

Here is an example of a letter to thank a keynote speaker—one whose speech you liked:

Dear Dr. Merriweather,

The moment you began to speak, it was clear that we made the right decision in choosing you to deliver the keynote address at our annual convention. Your speech was both entertaining and interesting, with just the right mix of hard data, examples, and opinions. Moreover, it was well-organized and easy to follow. I was especially impressed by the way you communicated your research results using the cleverly designed slides. All in all, you were a hit.

A number of people have asked for copies of the speech. Although it appeared that you weren't using notes, do you have a text of the speech you could share with us? If not, I'll understand.

Thank you for helping to make our annual conference such a resounding success. Your check for $1,000 is enclosed.

> Sincerely,
> Jacob Ornstein
> Program Chair

Volunteers

A thank-you note is the only "pay" volunteers receive for their effort—the only tangible proof that their efforts are valued. Even though a volunteer may believe he has made a valuable contribution, a written note of appreciation makes it "official." Moreover, the note you write creates a good impression, both for the organization you represent and for you as a leader. Volunteers whose efforts are clearly appreciated are more likely to volunteer again.

Send a thank-you note soon after the job has been completed, no matter how small. If the volunteer is involved with a large project, send the note after a major milestone has been completed. As with other business-related thank-you letters, avoid sending a form letter. Because a volunteer will want to know that you really noticed her work, be specific in your description of her contribution. Here's an example:

Dear Connie:

Thanks to your help and that of the other volunteers, the Spring Conference was an unquestioned success. We did it! We pulled it off with nary a hitch!

Your work with the Program Committee helped make the conference happen. Your time spent in meetings, phone calls and letter writing paid off with an exceptional line-up of speakers. Without an attractive program, a conference doesn't get very far.

Connie, steady workers like you are worth their weight in gold. I wish we could package your conscientiousness and thoroughness and so share it with all our chapter members.

Please enjoy the enclosed memento which is our thank you to you for a job exceptionally well done.

Sincerely,
Mary

This is an excellent example of a thank-you letter to a volunteer (me), for helping put on a regional conference for the Society for Technical Communication. The author is Mary Reilly McCall, who was then serving as conference coordinator.

Dear Margaret,

I don't know what we'd have done without your stalwart work heading up registration at our annual conference. Thanks to you, registration went smoothly and quickly, with no disgruntled people waiting in long lines. I know you had to do double duty when Joan became ill, and I want you to know that we all appreciate the extra effort you made to take up the slack.

As conference chairman, I am indebted to you and the others who worked so tirelessly to make our conference a success. The feedback we've been getting has been most heartening. I want you to know that people have been giving particularly high marks to our registration desk. I am so grateful to have you as part of our team. You are a treasure!

> Thanks again,
> Ernestine Sloan
> Conference Chair

A final word

Over the years, I've received numerous notes of thanks for volunteer work and for jobs well done. I have saved every one of these, even though I had no particular use for them—although once, when applying for a job, I created a sort of "what the critics are saying" anthology of excerpts from these letters as an addendum to my résumé. (I got the job.) As you write your thank-you notes to employees, customers, and others, bear in mind that your work may be around for a long, long time.

6

Discipline and Organization: How to Tackle Big Jobs

Tackling big jobs doesn't have to be overwhelming. The trick is to set little daily goals and stick with them. For example, each spring for about five years, I planted one hundred fruit trees on our small Michigan farm. Ten days before the trees were to arrive, I started digging ten holes a day. After that, planting the trees was easy. I used the same daily-goal technique for writing my wedding-gift thank-yous. (I even wrote them on my honeymoon, a behavior which, if not compulsive, certainly demonstrates a goal-oriented personality.)

Most of us rarely have to deal with big thank-you-note writing jobs. If you've had a big wedding, that occasion is most likely the only time you will need to write more than one hundred notes. A big funeral may be another occasion for writing lots of thank-you notes. But that's about it for your entire life.

Cathy Keating: An example for us all

If you have a big note-writing job ahead of you, begin by taking inspiration from Cathy Keating, the first lady of Oklahoma, who has probably written more thank-you notes in a week than most of us write in a lifetime.

Cathy and Governor Frank Keating held a statewide housewarming for the Oklahoma governor's mansion to establish a permanent collection of household articles, furnishings, and items of historical significance. Citizens from all over the state contributed items. Over the course of three months, Cathy Keating wrote a note to each donor—about 1,500 in all. She wrote and addressed each note by hand. I heard about Keating's feat on a National Public Radio interview and contacted her to find out more.

When I asked why she felt it was important to send a handwritten "customized" note to each donor rather than send the same generic note to all, she said she wanted "each donor to realize the significance of his or her contribution, not only to Frank and me (as Governor and First Lady), but also for Oklahoma's heritage. In essence, their thoughtfulness as well as time and money spent in purchasing the gift were well worth my time and energy to personally thank them." She also wanted the note to be appropriate to the sender. For example, the note she wrote to the second-grade class in Jenks, Oklahoma, was geared to that age group, whereas the note to the widow of an important Oklahoma entrepreneur emphasized the role the widow's husband had played in developing the state.

To accomplish the monumental task, Keating "spent every waking moment which was unscheduled writing notes." She wrote in the car, late into the night, and on her only day off.

It turned out that the 1,500 thank-you notes were just the beginning of Keating's note-writing efforts. "On the heels of the housewarming," she said, "came the Oklahoma City bombing. I also wrote hundreds, if not thousands, of personal handwritten notes to people all over the state, country, and world in response to the many offers of help and prayers and money." She wrote twenty-five to fifty notes a day "for months and months."

Cathy Keating's willingness to devote all her spare time to write personal and individualized thank-you notes to thousands of people demonstrates her belief that people deserve a heartfelt expression of gratitude in return for their kindness and generosity.

Thank-you-note horror stories

At the opposite end of the spectrum from Cathy Keating are people whose gratitude compass needs some adjustment, especially when it comes to wedding gifts. I read about a young man who had saved up enough money to attend his friend's wedding, which required an expensive plane trip. Because of his limited resources, he didn't send a gift. (He planned to save again until he could afford the purchase.) About seven months after the wedding, he received a note that said, "Thank you for sharing this special day with us. Thank you for your generosity except for the following people who did not send gifts." This sentence was followed by the names of everyone, including the young man, who did not send a gift.

In another case, a woman sent an expensive wedding gift to her husband's niece and received no acknowledgment. Over the course of several months, she wrote the bride three times, inquiring about the gift. She received no response to any of her letters. Finally, one year after the wedding, a note from the bride arrived. It was a birth announcement, at the bottom of which was written, "Thanks for the wedding gift." Understandably, the woman didn't dash out and buy a gift for the new baby. When a gift was not forthcoming, the new mother sent a postcard asking the woman if she was going to send a gift.

Sadly, these two cases represent the victory of greed over gratitude. In our society of ever-increasing abundance, this turn of mind appears to be on the increase. Instead of being grateful for the gifts we do receive, we complain about those we do not receive.

Strategies for wedding-gift thank-yous

As you contemplate writing thank-you notes for wedding gifts, think about your good fortune in receiving so many gifts. Approach the task as an opportunity to count your blessings instead of as an odious chore to be dreaded.

Admittedly, writing hundreds of thank-you notes takes time. But it is a very important activity. Each person who sent you a gift spent both time and money on your behalf. In return, you must express your gratitude for their generosity—and the sooner the better. At the least, gift-givers want an acknowledgment that you received the gift. They also want to know how you liked it.

You must figure out a way to get your wedding-gift thank-yous written quickly—ideally two weeks after the wedding or honeymoon. It's going to take some self-discipline. If, unlike Cathy Keating, you need help in that department, here are some suggestions:

🖋 *Get organized.* Before the wedding, as you gather addresses for your invitations, set up a file-card or notebook system in which you record the giver's name, address, occasion (shower or wedding), brief description of the gift, a "thank-you sent" check-box, and the date the thank-you was sent. Begin by recording each invitee's name and address. Then, as gifts arrive, record the remaining information—and begin writing the notes. This way, you'll keep track of the gifts as well as your thank-you notes. I know of one computer-savvy bride who used spreadsheet software to both track the information and also compose (and spell-check) her notes, which she then copied by hand. If you're opening a number of gifts on a single occasion, such as a shower, assign a family member the task of recording the gift and giver information on the file cards or in the notebook. Or you can tape each card to its gift and record the information later.

● *Start immediately*. There's no reason to wait until after the wedding to begin the job. Write your notes as soon as the gifts arrive. For example, if you receive three gifts in one day, write three thank-you notes that evening. In this way, you'll keep on top of the job instead of letting your duties pile up until you begin to feel overwhelmed. Plus, the recipient of your acknowledgment will be impressed.

● *One note at a time*. Don't think about the big writing job that lies ahead. Instead, imagine that the note you are writing at the moment is for the only gift you received. Think about the person who sent the gift, and direct your full attention to thanking that person for his or her kindness.

🍃 *Divide the job*. Share the workload with your partner. Divide the job in whatever way works best. For example, each partner could write to his or her friends and relatives. If one of you is a slacker, the other will simply have to take over. Don't nag or complain. Just get the job done.

🍃 *Set goals*. If, after the wedding, you still have many gifts to acknowledge, resolve to write a specific number of notes—say, ten—each day. Assuming each note takes three minutes to write, you can complete ten thank-yous in half an hour. You'll have one hundred thank-yous completed in ten days, well within the two-week time limit.

🍃 *Create a space*. Keep your paper, stamps, lists of gifts and addresses, and pen always at the ready. If you don't have a space you can devote solely to note writing, keep your supplies together in a box. Such a "portable desk" makes it easy to write notes while sitting in your easy chair during television commercials—or sitting on a rock near the ocean.

🍂 *Use "dead" time.* Write notes during the time of day that isn't typically devoted to some other task. For example, if you often spend some time after dinner thumbing through catalogs and magazines or talking on the phone, use that time instead to polish off some notes. Set aside that time as your nightly note-writing period. If you're a television watcher, write notes during commercials, or don't watch until you've accomplished your daily goal.

🍂 *Withhold gratification.* Don't allow yourself to use the wedding gift until after you've written and mailed the note. Better still, don't allow yourself to *open* a gift until you have written the note for the previously opened gift.

Debra Marrs, writing in *Bride's* magazine offers additional suggestions: Divide your gift list into categories, such as "your family, his family, and mutual friends" as a way of making the job seem less daunting. Write the difficult notes first to get them out of the way. Write for ten minutes, then, if you haven't wearied of the task, write for another ten minutes, and so on. Use the note writing as a time for "sharing, reminiscing, and planning" with your husband. Ask your maid of honor or mother to call and check on your progress.

Reward yourself after meeting a goal with a bubble bath or "snuggle with your husband in front of a roaring fire." When the entire job is completed, "splurge on an evening at the theater, an intimate dinner for two." (For me, finishing the job is reward enough! But you should choose whatever strategies will work for you.)

The perils of procrastination

If you delay or dodge your note-writing task, you'll feel badly, be embarrassed each time you meet one of the gift-givers, and acquire a reputation for rudeness. Besides, people might report your delinquency to your mother! One mother, embarrassed by her daughter's failure to write thank-you notes for wedding gifts, wrote and mailed the notes herself. The notes included this statement: "Please accept my apologies for her inexcusable negligence. I assure you, she wasn't raised that way." (I can imagine, with such a mother, the daughter might have a tendency toward rebellion.)

Don't even think about avoiding your written expressions of gratitude by using schemes such as handing out preprinted thank-you cards to each wedding guest or asking guests at your wedding shower to address their own thank-you envelopes or publishing your thanks in the newspaper. Not only are such strategies tacky in the extreme, but they demonstrate a stingy response to generosity.

The uses of acknowledgment cards

Some etiquette experts condone the use of a printed acknowledgment card for weddings that are very large or "public." (I assume by *public*, they mean something like that of Princess Diana and Prince Charles. But think of Cathy Keating!) If your wedding is very large and you are unable to send thank-you notes within a month after your honeymoon, then an acknowledgment card assures the giver that the present was received and that a proper thank-you note will follow. Here's an example of a printed acknowledgment card:

Diane Smith and Charles Jones
acknowledge with thanks
the receipt of your wedding gift and
will write you a personal note as soon as possible.

Unless your wedding is the size of Princess Diana's, I wouldn't recommend this strategy. It merely delays the job. Besides, it may lull you into thinking that you've thanked the gift-givers, which you haven't.

November 26 Tuesday

Dear Mr. President:

Thank you for walking yesterday—behind Jack. You did not have to do that—I am sure many people forbid you to take such a risk—but you did it anyway.

Thank you for your letters to my children. What those letters will mean to them later—you can imagine. The touching thing is, they have always loved you so much, they were most moved to have a letter from you now.

And most of all Mr. President, thank you for the way you have always treated me—the way you and Lady Bird have always been to me—before, when Jack was alive, and now as President.

I think the relationship of the Presidential and Vice Presidential families could be a rather strained one. From the history I have been reading ever since I came to the White House, I gather it often was in the past.

But you were Jack's right arm—and I always thought the greatest act of a gentleman that I had seen on this earth—was how you—the Majority Leader when he came to the Senate as just another little freshman who looked up to you and took orders from you, could then serve as Vice

President to a man who had served under you and been taught by you.

But more than that we were friends, all four of us. All you did for me as a friend and the happy times we had. I always thought way before the nomination that Lady Bird should be First Lady—but I don't need to tell you here what I think of her qualities—her extraordinary grace of character—her willingness to assume every burden—She assumed so many for me and I love her very much—and I love your two daughters—Lynda Bird most because I know her the best—and when we first met when neither of us could get a seat to hear President Eisenhower's State of the Union message and someone found us a place on one of the steps on the aisle where we sat together. If we had known then what our relationship would be now.

... It mustn't be very much help to you your first day in office—to hear children on the lawn at recess. It is just one more example of your kindness that you let them stay—I promise—they will soon be gone.

> Thank you Mr. President
> Respectfully
> Jackie

On the day after President John Kennedy's funeral, Jacqueline Kennedy wrote this thank-you letter to Lyndon Johnson.

If you receive three hundred gifts, you and your partner can each write 150 notes—ten a day each for fifteen days. However, if you simply cannot get your notes in the mail within a reasonable amount of time—say, a month—sending an acknowledgment card is better than nothing. But don't forget that you're still on the hook for that handwritten note.

Large funerals

If you are the person closest to someone whose death created an unusually large outpouring of flowers, charitable donations, letters, and cards, you can, if necessary, acknowledge each gesture with a preprinted card. Order such cards, usually white edged in black, with a simple expression such as

The family of Jonathan Bruce Westgate
greatly appreciates your kind expression of sympathy.

A handwritten note, of course, is always best. Even if you use the preprinted card, it is nice to write a brief note at the bottom of each card. Ask family members to help you with this job. The notes need not be sent as quickly as other types of thank-you notes; the traditional outside limit is six weeks after the funeral.

To keep track of who sent flowers, assign a family member to collect the attached cards and write a note on each that accurately describes the flowers and their arrangement. Charities to whom people have sent contributions in the deceased's name will inform you of each donation. Even though the donors will receive a note from the charity, you should also write a note.

Other gift-giving occasions

While weddings tend to be the occasions on which gifts arrive in abundance, other occasions, such as big anniversary, birthday, or bar mitzvah parties, may cause a similar deluge of gifts. In such cases, you'll need to keep track of gifts and their donors just as you would for wedding gifts. You may even need a tracking system at Christmas or Chanukah. For example, if you have a large family gathering at Christmas or Chanukah with gifts being opened in the usual happy chaos—and if some of the gifts come from long-distance friends or relatives—you can save yourself potential embarrassment by adopting a method to keep track of who gave what. One obvious method is to simply keep a pad of paper handy and jot down the name of the giver and a description of the gift. As one friend who uses this method said to me, "We've all learned the hard way that it's easy to lose track of who gave what when there's so much, and it's embarrassing to have to write, 'I hope I haven't left anything out.'"

Published thanks

Peggy Post says, "In certain localities, most especially small towns and rural areas, it is not only permissible but expected that recipients of a large number of gifts or kindness put a public 'thanks' in the paper." Occasions that merit this type of thanks, she says, include "funerals, retirement parties, anniversary parties, birthdays, political campaigns, professional advancements, and any other events that result in special kindnesses, assistance, gifts or contributions." Ms. Post adds that if you do this, it isn't necessary to send written thanks, although she does suggest that you send written thanks to people who have gone "out of their way to give something very special."

Except in very small towns and rural areas, I can't imagine a locale where the newspaper-published thanks will suffice as an acceptable expression of gratitude. The only exceptions may be the offering of thanks from a public person, such as an elected official, acknowledging his or her supporters; or from an

Concord, July 29, 1872

Dear Sir — I desire to express to you, and through you to the engineers and members of the Fire Department of this town, the sincere thanks of myself and each one of my family for the able, hearty and in great measure successful exertion in our behalf in resisting and extinguishing the fire which threatened to destroy my house on Wednesday morning last. We owe it to your efficient labor and skill that so large a part of the building was saved, and let me say that we owe it to your families and a great number of generous volunteers that almost all the furniture, clothing, and especially the books and papers contained in the house were saved and removed with tender care. I hope to have the opportunity of thanking, sooner or later, every one of our benefactors in person.

Yours most gratefully,
R. W. Emerson

In 1872, Ralph Waldo Emerson's home caught fire. This letter, which was addressed to J. C. Sanborn, chief-engineer of the Concord Fire Department, was published in the Concord newspaper.

organization, such as the volunteer fire department, thanking the community for its support; or from an individual or family thanking a rescuer or good Samaritan whose name was never learned.

But if you're certain that the folks in your town would be disappointed not to see your note of gratitude published in the newspaper, it's OK to do it. My local paper frequently publishes letters of thanks, but usually only for expressing appreciation to the public at large for support of some event or cause or to publicly acknowledge the good work of the fire department after coming to the rescue. In fact, such published thanks helps to publicize worthy causes and to bestow credit on deserving people and institutions.

7

Training and Education: How to Get Children to Write Thank-You Notes

etitia Baldrige says, "A child should send a thank-you note (or a young child's parent should write on his behalf) to thank for presents, parties attended, and having been asked to 'spend the night.' If a child forms this habit early he will carry it through his life, and will find that his good manners will always be one of his greatest assets."

That's easier said than done.

Getting my kids to write thank-you notes was always hard for me. I had no clever strategies or motivating schemes. Mostly I nagged. I'd also threaten "no dinner." I can't remember how successful that strategy was; I know no one starved.

Some of my kids wrote notes; some didn't. Because some didn't, my mother, like many grandmothers before and since, quit sending gifts to all five of my children, the writers and nonwriters alike. She painted them all with the same no-gift brush. (What else could she do?) One of my daughters, now in her forties, still prickles at the injustice of it all.

You *can* get kids to write thank-you notes. Others have been successful.

It will take time and dedication, at least at first. But in the end, you'll have well-trained, well-mannered, and thoughtful children.

Dear Gramma,

    You are rely nice to sen me the red truk. It goes fast and krashes rely wham. I love you Gramma. You sure no yur truks.

A proud grandmother saved this note and passed it along to Letitia Baldrige, who included it in her Complete Guide to the New Manners for the '90s.

Why the training is important

I think Judith Martin is right when she says that, unless trained to do so, people may go "merrily through life without ever having pondered the relationship between gifts and gratitude." Small children, by their nature, enjoy their presents without feelings of gratitude to those who gave them. For this reason, they must be taught that presents are not just acquisitions but gestures of kindness and generosity. Through training, children can learn to associate gratitude with generosity. In fact, it's a rare child who just naturally takes to writing thank-you notes. If you want your children to be thoughtful and courteous, you must knuckle under and apply yourself to the task of training your children—preferably at a preliterate age—whether they like it or not.

Beginning early

To make note writing a habit, start when the kids are young and enthusiastic about helping perform "grown-up" tasks. When your children are too young to write, the notes should be from you. By age three, a child can be made aware that a thank-you note is being written on his or her behalf.

Dear Aunt Connie,

Thank you for the ring game and the coloring book. I like them both, even though I do like the ring game.

p.s. Here in San Diego it does not seem like winter.

Siened Joe Ludlow

My nephew Joe Ludlow, when he was around eight, wrote this thank-you note on Cub Scout stationery. Note that he followed the spelling rule: i before e except after c.

You can initiate your child into note writing in a number of ways:

- *Write the note yourself, with your child's participation.* Sit down with your child and tell him you are writing a note to thank Aunt Molly for the gift. Ask him to tell you what he likes about the gift and then write what he says. For example, "Billy loves the action figures you sent. He says he 'likes all the stuff they can do.'" If your child is old enough, he can sign his name. If he can't, sign your own name. He can also draw a picture, add decorative stamps, or write Xs and Os on the note.

- *Have the child draw and dictate.* Your child can draw a picture about her gift and dictate a message for you to add. Or she can dictate the letter and decorate it with stamps. Or she can sit with you as you create a card on the computer.

- *Have the child copy a note you write.* If your child has learned the rudiments of writing but cannot create sentences without some help, she can copy something you write but that has been dictated by her: "Dear Grandma, Thank you for the dress. I like it. Love, Patsy."

- *Take photos.* Some parents take snapshots of their child holding both the gift and a big "Thank You"

Dear Grandma,

Last night I went to a spice girls concert! It was so fun! Thanck you for the stationary! I Love It. how is your Summer going? Mine is fine.

Lov Maggie

P.S. I love the earrings!

One of my granddaughters, Maggie Stoody, at around age eight, sent me this thank-you in response to a birthday gift.

sign. The photo thus serves as the "note." In a similar—though more effortful vein—I have read about parents who take a photo of everyone who attended the birthday party. They then make photocopies and add a note at the bottom. One mother writes poems instead of notes. (This demonstrates her cleverness, but I think the effect is one of mass production.) Another mother has the photocopy center create postcards from the party photos, and then she adds notes to each. Even more elaborate, one mother takes snapshots of her child playing with each gift after the party, and then she inserts the photos into paper frames and writes thank-yous around the edges. Ideally, for the sake of the child's training, the child should participate in all such endeavors.

> *Be an example.* Because children learn by example, casually point out when you are writing a note yourself. A welfare recipient, having been featured in an article about welfare to work, received money from sympathetic readers. Three years later, in a follow-up article, she expressed deep regrets at never having sent notes of thanks to the donors, recognizing that her behavior set a poor example for her children: "It's hard to tell your kids things when you don't practice it."

After the child can write

For a beginning writer, a sentence or two will do. You can help by addressing the envelope. After a child becomes a better writer, say by age eight, he should be able to manage two or three sentences, but you should probably still write the address. As the child's handwriting improves, he should take care of the complete project including the note, address, and stamp. Be ready to help when your child asks questions, such as how to spell a word, but avoid correcting and editing his work. Instead, offer praise and encouragement.

After your child is really writing, teach him the basic structure:

1. The salutation. ("Dear Aunt Martha.")
2. The body of the note, including a "thank you" sentence, which mentions the gift, plus a sentence that comments on the gift—preferably what she likes about it. ("Thank you for the Parcheesi game. It's really fun to play.")
3. A closing sentence, which can be anything from a newsy message to an "I love you."
4. The complimentary close plus signature. ("Love, Margaret" or "Your friend, Sam.")

Remind your child that gift-givers need to be acknowledged for their thoughtfulness even if the present wasn't to his liking. For such cases, prompt your child to describe the qualities of the gift. By focusing on qualities ("Red is my favorite color") as opposed to how well he likes it, he can thank the giver without being dishonest. For gifts of money, your child should tell what he plans to do with it, even if he's planning to save it. Encourage your child to send the notes promptly. Procrastination makes the thank-you seem unimportant, both to your child and to the recipient.

Strategies for success

It is a rare child who willingly—and without prodding—writes thank-you notes. The nagging technique, many of us have found, is both tiresome for everyone concerned as well as of questionable utility. Some clever parents have been successful using the following techniques:

> 🖐 *Prepare kids in advance.* Before the holidays or birthday, one mother takes her children to pick out the stamps, stationery, and a special pen. She reserves these items for thank-you notes. She then determines, with the children's help, a good

day to work on the notes and marks the day on the family calendar. Then she sets out the writing supplies on that day.

🐾 *Make it fun.* Buy colorful and fun note cards, pens, and stickers. Provide a special place for writing as well as snacks or rewards for a job well done.

🐾 *Organize, then chip away.* One mother of four sits down with her children the day after Christmas and makes a list of all who need to be thanked. She then provides her children with supplies and encourages them to chip away at the job until it's done—but it needn't be in one sitting. She doesn't force it. Her only rule is "Just so it's not embarrassingly late."

🐾 *Tackle the chore together.* Sit with your child as she writes her notes, perhaps writing your own notes at the same time. Make suggestions only if the child asks, and don't fuss over or edit spelling and grammar. These will come later. Praise her after each note.

🐾 *Create incentives.* Promise your children that on the day the notes are completed, they will get a special treat, such as a family night at the movies.

🐾 *Use preprinted cards.* One mother buys preprinted thank-you cards that have just enough

Hi grandma its me stephanie I just wanted
to say THANKS for your wonderful halloween
present!!!!!!!!!!!!!!!!!!!!that you sent me!!!!!!!!!!!
I can not wait to see you for thanksgiving!!
iam so excited.
Oh yea and I also can wate to put on that
nailpolesh you sent me.

Well I have to go now so talk to you later by
LOVE YOU

P.S tell grandpa i said hi and i love him to.

LOVE Stephanie

This message, which was e-mailed, is from another
granddaughter of mine, Stephanie Wiesen. Exuberant,
I would call it.

space for one sentence from a beginning writer. This strategy gives a child the feeling of accomplishment.

🖋 *Use fill-in-the-blanks cards.* Some parents create a set of fill-in-the-blanks thank-you notes with this text: "Dear_____. Thank you so much for the _____. I really like it because_____. Your friend _____." I suppose this strategy is better than nothing, and it does teach the basic structure of a note, but I wouldn't encourage my children to send "form letters."

🖋 *Create computer-generated cards.* Computer-savvy children can use greeting-card software to create their own cards. Or they can use Internet sites (such as *bluemountain.com* or *e-cards.com*) to send e-mail cards. You must ensure, however, that each card includes a message which mentions the gift and what the child likes about it.

🖋 *Trade chores for notes.* Allow the child to trade a chore for writing a note. For example, instead of setting the table, the child writes a note.

🖋 *Withhold the gift.* Some parents do not allow their children to play with or otherwise use a gift until the note is in the mail. One mother, who successfully uses this strategy, says that she explained to her two boys that "people who care enough to send gifts deserve reciprocal care, and it is certainly not fair for them to be denied gratitude for their generosity." Her children have one week to accomplish their task, after which the gift will go back to the sender. "I have never had to make good on that threat . . . but I will do so if necessary," she says, adding that her two boys "write their notes faithfully within one or two days with only a minimal reminder."

🍃 *Re-create the purchase.* One mother became weary of nagging her children to write thank-yous. She tried withholding the gifts until her children had written the notes, but still they procrastinated. So she decided to impress on her children the time and effort required to purchase, wrap, and mail a gift by enacting the tasks, beginning with a shopping trip. One child kept track of the time required to drive to the store, shop, wrap, and drive to the post office. The job took two hours and thirty-four minutes. Thus chastened, her children then each wrote their notes, following her instructions to "mention the present by name and tell what fun you'll have using it." It took them three minutes. The strategy has continued to work.

What grandparents and other "outsiders" can do

One method that grandparents commonly use when thank-you notes are not forthcoming is to cease sending gifts. Or you could have a friendly talk with your grandchild, saying that you always try to please him or her, but because you received no response for the present, you must assume that you missed the mark. When the child protests, you then stress the importance of feedback to keep the gifts coming. Another strategy, aimed at older children who have been negligent, is to omit the present and send only a note of greetings and other chitchat. Then at the end of the letter, say that you haven't sent the usual presents because you assume their lack of response to previous gifts indicates that you have not been successful at finding something to please them. If you prefer a more direct approach, you can, like George and Barbara Bush, simply call your grandchildren and complain if a thank-you note hasn't arrived within a suitable time.

When the child does send a thank-you note, be sure to mention how pleased you were to get it. In some cases, you might even consider writing a thank-you in return for the child's note. While a thank-you note doesn't normally require a thank-you note in

Dear Uncle Arthur,

   I am writing this to you as I sit under the hair dryer at the beauty salon. Tonight is the Holiday Ball at the high school and I am spending your Christmas check having my hair done for the party.
   Thank you very much. I know I'll have a wonderful time, in part because of your thoughtful gift.

                     Love,
                     Faith

Faith Andrews Bedford, writing in Country Living *magazine, discovered that her great uncle, who had sent her $5.00 each Christmas, had saved all the thank-you notes she had written to him as a child and teenager. This is one of them.*

return, if a child has taken the trouble to write to you, a word of appreciation in response provides a reward for good behavior.

I heard about a grandmother who saves all her grandchildren's thank-you notes. After the children are grown, she puts the notes together in a little booklet and gives it to them as a gift. Needless to say, after receiving such a treasure, the recipients of these booklets are glad they wrote their notes. Both grandmother and grandchildren have the pleasure of seeing, as in a series of photographs, the changes brought by the passage of time.

Is sincerity required?

"It is dreadful to teach children to feign emotions," writes a woman to Miss Manners. It would seem that many people share this opinion—and not only as it applies to children. David Owen is one of them. Writing in *The New Yorker* magazine, he says, "The gratitude of others is most pleasing when it does not seem to be a mere side effect of a brutally disciplined upbringing.... The only way to cultivate this sense of spontaneity—fortunately—is to be stingy with one's gratefulness." Owen would do away with thank-you notes.

William McGurn, a columnist for *The Wall Street Journal*, observes that the people who don't send thank-yous outnumber those who do. "The decline of the thank-you note," he writes, "can be attributed to the corresponding elevation of sincerity. Sincerity is not always called for, especially when you're five years old and Aunt Martha got you a new itchy sweater in exactly the wrong color instead of the Pokemon cards you were hoping for. Even adults know that the obligations of gratitude are such that they override the usual imperative for truthfulness."

Truthfulness is not the important thing here. What is important is that the child learns to be polite, an aspect of early childhood training that leads to morality. "Politeness," writes Comte-Sponville, "is a small thing that paves the way for great things. To say 'thank you' is to pretend to be grateful. And it is with this show of respect and this show of gratitude that both respect and gratitude begin.... It is by mimicking the ways of virtue, that is, through politeness, that we stand a chance of becoming virtuous." And finally, "Politeness is not everything; indeed it is almost nothing. *Almost*, but not quite: for man, too, is *almost* an animal."

To the woman who opined that children shouldn't be taught to "feign emotions," Miss Manners responded that parents who do not teach their children the amenities must therefore "want the child to remain in the natural, and therefore uncivilized, state in which he was born...." This is an overstatement, of course. We all want our children to behave in a civilized manner. But the training is hard work—especially when it comes to getting kids to write thank-you notes.

8

Self and Others:
How Writing Thank-You
Notes Can Enlarge
the Spirit

Whether your thank-you notes are motivated by feelings of guilt, a sense of duty, etiquette concerns, or an outpouring of gratitude, the results of your work can have consequences you never imagined.

An antidote to greed

To begin with, thank-you notes can help ameliorate a self-centered approach to life, as exemplified by a person who wrote to Ann Landers: "I think thank-you notes are a lot of hooey. People who have dreadful taste don't deserve to be thanked. Consider the husband who buys his wife a log-splitter on her birthday, or the diabetic who receives chocolates on Valentine's Day, or the vegetarian who is sent a 'meat-of-the-month' package." In this view, gift-givers deserve words of appreciation only if the recipient is 100 percent satisfied. The time, effort, and good intentions of the donor are nothing compared to the desires of the receiver. What matters is that I get what I want. My feelings count; yours don't.

I hope this point of view is not shared by anyone but that writer. But I suspect his outlook may be widely held. Judging at least by accounts of brides and grooms who are hell-bent on getting what they want—and often this is money—it appears that our greed may be outdistancing our gratitude. (I heard of

Dear Connie,

Walking along the path of the Elkhorn Slough, binoculars in hand, tried-and-true friend at my side, I felt uniquely privileged to be in that place at the time with you. This is a thank-you note for that experience and for all the others that you provided.

I also want to mention your home. Your mother would be astonished at the beauty of the place. Commonplace to you because you are there all the time but extraordinary to me. I hope to come back at some time with a really good camera and do it justice. It invites photographic challenges. I have in mind a kind of photographic essay with you in your old age and the house in the flush of its maturity: Connie as Georgia and Casa Margarita as Ghost Ranch. Maybe I will even be able to invent a new metaphor by that time. . . .

Walking along the path of old friendship I find that I treasure it just as we did the Elkhorn. Two old birds still paddling about, honking cordially in mutual contentment. This old bird thanks you very much for a wonderful visit. Will send pictures when ready.

> With love and friendship,
> Your tried-and-true friend
> Susan

I received this letter from my former college room-mate—a friend now for more than forty-five years—who spent two nights as a guest in our home. Among other things, I took her for a walk in a local wildlife sanctuary.

155

one couple who held a money-raising auction at their wedding reception.)

By taking the time to sit down and write a note of thanks, the focus of our attention switches from self to the other. At least for a moment, our own desires are set aside as we begin to express appreciation for the generosity of others.

A spiritual discipline

Writing thank-you notes can also help us experience a sense of gratitude in our everyday lives. I have a friend whose middle-aged, well-educated daughter doesn't acknowledge gifts because she doesn't like to feel "obligated." In my dictionary, the definition for *oblige* is "to make indebted or grateful." "Oblige" does sound burdensome; so does "indebted." But as Oscar Wilde discovered during his time of imprisonment, joy can be found in counting up what you owe, not in what you own. In a thank-you letter to Max Beerbohm (1897), he writes,

> *I used to think gratitude a heavy burden for one to carry. Now I know that it is something that makes the heart lighter. The ungrateful man seems to me to be one who walks with feet and heart of lead. But*

*when one has learnt, however inadequately, what a
lovely thing gratitude is, one's feet go lightly over
sand or sea, and one finds a strange joy revealed to
one, the joy of counting up, not what one possesses,
but what one owes. I hoard my debts now in the
treasury of my heart, and, piece of gold by piece
of gold, I range them in order at dawn and at
evening. So you must not mind my saying that
I am grateful to you. It is simply one of certain
new pleasures that I have discovered.*

As Wilde realized, being grateful can make you
aware of your blessings and thankful for them. Some
people, at Oprah Winfrey's suggestion, have started
keeping a "gratitude journal" for the practice of everyday thankfulness. In addition to making us aware of
our blessings, practicing everyday thankfulness can,
according to Comte-Sponville, prolong the pleasure
that caused us to be grateful in the first place, "like a
joyful echo of the joy we feel, a further happiness for
the happiness we have been given." Gratitude, he
adds, is "a state of grace."

A friend of mine introduced me to Dawn Price, a
remarkable woman who does Oprah one better: She
writes and sends a thank-you note *every day*. Doing so
makes her feel "centered and happy" and reminds her

28 April 1900

Dear Sir I wish to thank you for your kindness in writing to me. I am a young Irishman, eighteen year old, and the words of Ibsen I shall keep in my heart all my life.

Faithfully yours
Jas A. Joyce

This is author James Joyce's expression of gratitude to playwright Henrik Ibsen (via Ibsen's translator) for Ibsen's complimentary words about a piece Joyce had written.

that she is a lucky person. The recipients of her notes are clearly thrilled to receive them, as evidenced by the fact that the notes are frequently on display. For example, a note she wrote to her printer in appreciation for good work ended up framed and hung in the front office.

Ms. Price writes notes of appreciation to anyone to whom she feels gratitude. "My best notes," she says, "come when I realize I haven't written a note that day and have to think a bit about whom to write. Those tend, then, to be thank-yous for less obvious things. For example, I might write a note to a co-worker thanking her for support on a project, or to the librarian at my son's school to let her know how much he is enjoying his library books." This practice of taking time each day to express thanks not only rewards the recipient with unexpected recognition but also serves as a kind of spiritual discipline for the writer.

Catherine Calvert, writing in *Town and Country* magazine, says that writing thank-you notes "can be one of life's purest pleasures, in which the truly imaginative transmute the 'chore' into something special— the most basic form of communication, heart to heart.

"Without a thank-you," she adds, "the cycle of giving is incomplete. Something pleasurable—but also something fundamental—is lost when expedience is chosen over form. If poetry is emotion recollected in tranquility, then surely a gesture of thanks can be a perfect poem."

A new habit

It doesn't matter whether or not you've been remiss in sending thank-you notes in the past. It's never too late to start. Don't worry about your writing skills or your penmanship. (Mine is awful.) And try not to make note writing an onerous chore. Rather, spend your writing time focusing on the person who deserves your thanks and perhaps even contemplating the good things in your life. You may also find you enjoy the creative aspect of writing—choosing just the right words to convey your feelings. As a bonus, you may even discover that sitting down with pen and paper is a stress-reliever, an activity that helps you slow down and enjoy a few moments of quiet.

Even if you don't exploit note writing as a time for spiritual renewal or to flex your creative muscles, getting into the habit of writing thank-you notes is easy to do. Get yourself some stationery or note cards that please you, a pen that you like, and a supply of stamps. Then, the next time someone does something that you appreciate, take two minutes to write him or her a note. The recipients of your notes will be grateful—and probably impressed. Also, don't worry if you've been derelict in your note-writing duties. You can start your new habit now. Others will appreciate your thoughtfulness and you'll quickly slough off the guilt from past negligence.

Who knows what your new note-writing habit will bring? You might just start a trend among your friends and relatives. By becoming a regular writer of thank-you notes, you can even help restore some civility to our digitally distressed society. As Cathy Keating said, writing notes of thanks is the right thing to do.

Appendix

Words and phrases to use in thank-you notes

Phrases to say thank you

thank you so much

thank you for remembering

many thanks

both send our thanks

deeply/truly/really appreciate

can't thank you enough

thanks a million

am/are so grateful

special thanks to...

particularly grateful because...

Words to describe things and events

appropriate	delightful	favorite
attractive	elegant	glamorous
beautiful	entertaining	handsome
charming	exquisite	ideal
decorative	fascinating	impressive

lovely
magnificent
memorable
much-needed
one-of-a-kind
perfect
pretty

remarkable
satisfying
sensational
special
stunning
superb
terrific

treasure
treat
unique
useful
valuable
versatile
wonderful

Words to describe feelings

admire
affection
appreciate
delighted
enchanted
enjoyed
flattered

grateful
happy
impressed
indebted
love
moved
overjoyed

overwhelmed
pleased
stunned
surprised
thrilled
touched

Words to describe people

clever
dear
generous/generosity
gracious
hospitable/hospitality
kind/kindness
talented
thoughtful/thoughtfulness

Phrases for gifts

conversation piece
delighted to receive
distinctive accessory
enjoy using
exactly what we wanted
excellent idea
fun to use
just what I/we need
just what I/we wanted
perfect choice

perfect for any occasion
perfect for entertaining
perfect match for
place of honor
plan to use it for
terrific idea
welcome addition to
will always treasure
will think of you

Phrases to express gratitude for hospitality

a great pleasure to spend time
delicious/luscious food
delightful evening
enjoyed myself/ourselves
   enormously
great/stimulating
   conversations
nice break

rare treat
still talking about
such fun
thoroughly enjoyed
very much enjoyed
will always
   remember
will never forget

Phrases to express gratitude for condolences

I/we appreciate your
   compassion
   condolences

kind words/remarks
love and support during this difficult time
standing by me
taking the time
thoughtful expression of sympathy
helped me get through
know how much you care
more important than you may know

When to send thank-you notes

Occasion	Must? Should? Nice to?
Wedding gifts, whether opened in front of giver or not	Must
Wedding attendants and all others who helped	Should
Other-occasion gift, opened in front of giver	Nice to; but should if gift is serious
Other-occasion gift, not opened in front of giver	Must unless thank-you is phoned; should if gift serious; always nice to

Occasion	*Must? Should? Nice to?*
Child's birthday-party gift	Nice to; must if giver is absent from party
Overnight stay as guest in someone's home	Must
Parties and dinners hosted by others	Should; must if you're the guest of honor; always nice to
Acts of kindness	Should
Good service and helpfulness	Should
Funeral flowers and condolence letters	Must
Sympathy cards	Nice to
All who helped with funeral	Must
Job well done	Should
Business referral	Should
Job interview	Must—if you want the job

Types of paper and formats for thank-you notes

Form	Uses
Social stationery (white folded note paper with monogram) or correspondence cards	The most "socially correct" form and paper; traditionally used for formal weddings; appropriate for nearly all occasions except letters destined for someone's personnel file; should always be handwritten
"Ordinary" folded note cards, decorated or not	Appropriate for all occasions except letters destined for someone's personnel file; should always be handwritten
Typewritten on stationery	For business-style thank-you notes, especially those thanking employees for a job well done or to acknowledge exceptional service by a business or governmental employee

Form	*Uses*
E-mail messages	Rarely acceptable, but better than nothing; may be OK for informal notes of appreciation to co-workers
E-cards (available from Internet businesses and sent electronically)	Rarely acceptable, but better than nothing
Faxed messages	Acceptable only if recipient lives in a remote place with iffy postal service and no e-mail
Preprinted commercial card	Acceptable if you include a handwritten message

Bibliography

Selected Letters

Bush, George H. *All the Best, George Bush: My Life in Letters and Other Writings*. New York: Lisa Drew/Scribner, 1999.

Emerson, Ralph Waldo. *The Selected Letters of Ralph Waldo Emerson*. Edited by Joel Meyerson. New York: Columbia University Press, 1997.

Grunwald, Lisa, and Stephen J. Adler, eds. *Letters of the Century: America, 1900–1999*. New York: The Dial Press, 1999.

Hanff, Helene. *Eighty-Four, Charing Cross Road*. New York: The Viking Press, Grossman Publishers, 1975.

Hemingway, Ernest. *Ernest Hemingway: Selected Letters, 1917–1961*. Edited by Carlos Baker. New York: Charles Scribner's Sons, 1981.

Joyce, James. *Selected Letters of James Joyce*. Edited by Richard Ellman. New York: The Viking Press, 1975.

Marx, Groucho. *The Groucho Letters*. New York: Simon and Schuster, 1967.

Moore, Marianne. *The Selected Letters of Marianne Moore*. Edited by Bonnie Costello. New York: Alfred A. Knopf, 1997.

O'Connor, Flannery. *Flannery O'Connor: The Habit of Being*. Edited by Sally Fitzgerald. New York: Farrar Straus and Giroux, 1979.

O'Neill, Eugene. *Selected Letters of Eugene O'Neill*. Edited by Travis Bogard and Jackson R. Bryer. New Haven, Conn.: Yale University Press, 1988.

Wilde, Oscar. *Selected Letters of Oscar Wilde*. Edited by Rupert Hart-Davis. Oxford: Oxford University Press, 1979.

References

Baldrige, Letitia. *Letitia Baldrige's Complete Guide to the New Manners for the '90s*. New York: Macmillan, 1990.

———, ed. *The Amy Vanderbilt Complete Book of Etiquette*. New York: Doubleday, 1978.

Bride's magazine, eds. *Bride's Book of Etiquette*. 5th ed. New York: Putnam Publishing, 1984.

Comte-Sponville, Andrè. *A Small Treatise on the Great Virtues*. New York: Metropolitan Books, 2001.

Fox, Sue. *Etiquette for Dummies*. Foster City, Calif.: IDG Books Worldwide, 1999.

———, and Perrin Cunningham. *Business Etiquette for Dummies*. Foster City, Calif.: IDG Books Worldwide, 2001.

Goodwin, Gabrielle, and David Macfarlane. *Writing Thank-You Notes*. New York: Sterling, 1999.

Henderson, Bill, ed. *Minutes of the Lead Pencil Club: Pulling the Plug on the Electronic Revolution*. New York: Pushcart Press, 1996.

Martin, Judith. *Miss Manners' Guide to Domestic Tranquility*. New York: Random House, 1999.

———. *Miss Manners' Guide for the Turn-of-the-Millennium*. New York: Pharos Books, 1989.

Phillips, Ellen. *Shocked, Appalled, and Dismayed!* New York: Vintage Books, 1997.

Piljac, Pamela A. *The Bride's Thank You Guide*. Chicago: Chicago Review Press, 1988.

Post, Peggy. *Emily Post's Etiquette*. 16th ed. New York: HarperCollins, 1997.

Maggio, Rosalie. *How to Say It*. Paramus, N.J.: Prentice Hall, 1990.

Poe, Roy W. *The McGraw-Hill Handbook of Business Letters*. 3rd ed. New York: McGraw-Hill, 1983.

Stewart, Marjabelle Young, with Elizabeth Lawrence. *Commonsense Etiquette: A Guide to Gracious, Simple Manners for the Twenty-First Century*. New York: St. Martin's, Griffin, 1999.

Wagman, Cat. *Why . . . Thank You!* Pembroke Pines, Fla.: Working Words, 1997.

Newspaper and Magazine Articles

Bedford, Faith Andrews. "A New Attitude to Gratitude." *Reader's Digest*, January 2000, 118.

Bodnar, Janet, and Marc L. Schulhof. "Dr. Tightwad Talks to Grandparents." *Kiplinger's Personal Finance Magazine*, May 1995, 95.

Brownell, Eileen O. "How to Make Yourself Memorable." *American Salesman*, June 1999, 11.

Calvert, Catherine. "Say Thank You." *Town and Country*, May 1997, 98.

DeParle, Jason. "Welfare to Work: A Sequel." *The New York Times Magazine*, December 28, 1999, 14.

Dobkin, Jeffrey. "The Most Valuable Letter You Can Write." *American Salesman*, January 1999, 27.

Dunninger, Irma, and Ruth Ann Stump. "Thanks a Lot." *Child Life*, December 1994 , 12.

Fisher, Anne. "How Do I Say Thanks for the Options? . . . What's the Netiquette for an Online Job Search." *Fortune*, March 1998, 174.

Flatt, Carolyn, and L. K. Williams. "Business Etiquette: A Competitive Edge." *CPA Journal*, July 1995, 12.

Hartsook, Robert F. "Thank the Donor 'Seven Times.'" *Fund Raising Management*, April 2000, 34.

Himmel, Sheila. "Feaster's Famine." *West*, June 1, 1997, 36.

"Holiday Thank-Yous." *Better Homes and Gardens*, September 22, 1999.

Kaufman, Joanne. "I Gave at the Office." *New York*, January 21–28, 2002, 28–29.

Marrs, Debra. "How to Say Thanks in Six Weeks or Less." *Bride's*, February/March 1992, 310.

Maude, Michael R. "On Gratitude." *Fund Raising Management*, September 1999, 32.

McGurn, William. "Thanks for Reading This." *The Wall Street Journal*, November 26, 1999.

Miles, Karen. "Thank You." *Woman's Day*, November 16, 1999, 78.

Morris, Mary. "Why ... Thank You!" *McCall's*, December 1999, 56.

Mynatt, Karen. "Write Thank-You Notes with the Kids." *Woman's Day*, January 10, 1995, 24.

The New York Times, eds. "Mail Call." *The New York Times*, May 19, 1994.

Owen, David. "No Thanks." *The New Yorker*, December 18, 1995.

Perle, Ann. "Have an Attitude of Gratitude." *Workforce*, November 1997, 77.

Post, Peggy. "Good Manners." *Parents*, September 1998, 168.

———. "Etiquette for Today." *Good Housekeeping*, December 1999, 47.

Rensenbrink, Kathryn. "Of Pretzels and Fruitcake: The Tales of a Rural Doctor." *The New York Times*, November 21, 2000.

Robinson, Roxana. "Great Expectations." *The New York Times Magazine*, June 17, 2001, 86.

Rommelman, Nancy. "Cosmo's Ten Commandments." *Cosmopolitan*, May 1998, 174.

Rosenthal, Amy Krouse. "Make Thank-You Notes Fun." *Redbook*, October 1999, 179.

Rubin, Richard. "Sorryyourdogdied.com." *Newsweek*.

Schwartz, Maryln. "Did You Thank Mom for the Advice?" *San Jose Mercury News*, February 23, 2001.

Scott, David Clark. "Tardy Thanks." *The Christian Science Monitor*, January 6, 1999, 13.

Sheehan, George. "Giving Thanks." *Runner's World*, May 1995, 20.

Singer, Karl. "A Piece of Cake." *Patient Care*, April 30, 2000.

Smolen, Wendy, and Amy Leonard. "Let's Party," *Parents*, May 1999, 153.

Stanffacher, Sue. "Holiday Thank-Yous." *Better Homes and Gardens*, January 1998, 44.

Stryker, Mark. "Orchestra's Thank-You Notes Spur Woman in Nursing Home to Give $2.5 Million." *Detroit Free Press*, November 17, 1999.

Wald, Catherine S. "So Many Ways to Say Thank You." *Woman's Day*, November 19, 1996, 44.

———. "Gracious Thanks: How to Write Memorable Notes." *Bride's*, June/July 1991.

Wambrunn, Susan. "Encouraging Words Keep Clergy's Spirits Up." *San Jose Mercury News*, October 14, 2000. Reprinted from the *Gazette* (Colorado Springs).

Internet References

Carliner, Sue. "Thank You Notes: The Volunteer's Paycheck." *web.bentley.edu/empl/c/scarliner/thankyounotes.htm*. Reprinted with permission from *Tieline*, the newsletter of the Society for Technical Communication (Arlington, Virginia), © 2000.

Hinds, Jean and Noe Spaemme. "Thank You Notes from Hell." *www.etiquettehell.com*.

Minnesota Department of Economic Security. "Creative Job Search." *www.mnworkforcecenter.org*.

The State University of New York, University at Buffalo. "Thank You Notes." *www.ub-careers.buffalo.edu*.

Permissions

The author gratefully acknowledges permission from the following to reprint material in this book:

Alfred A. Knopf, a division of Random House, Inc., for a letter from Marianne Moore to Louise Crane (p. 381) from *The Selected Letters of Marianne Moore*, by Marianne Moore, edited by Bonnie Costello, copyright © by the Estate of Marianne Moore and © 1997 by Bonnie Costello.

Farrar Straus and Giroux, LLC, for a letter from Flannery O'Connor to William Sessions, December 27, 1956 (p. 189) from *Flannery O'Connor: The Habit of Being*, edited by Sally Fitzgerald, copyright © 1979 by Regina O'Connor.

The New York Times for "Mail Call," May 19, 1994, copyright © 1994 by *The New York Times*.

Scribner, a division of Simon & Schuster, Inc., for a letter from George Bush to Ms. Goldie Hawn (p. 526) from *All the Best, George Bush: My Life in Letters and Other Writings*, by George Bush, copyright © 1999 by George H. W. Bush.

Scribner for excerpts of letters by Ernest Hemingway to Grace Hall Hemingway (pp. 4–5) and to John and Katharine Dos Passos (p. 433) from *Ernest Hemingway: Selected*

Letters, 1917–1961, edited by Carlos Baker, copyright ©
1981 by The Ernest Hemingway Foundation, Inc.

Simon and Schuster for letters from Groucho Marx to
Betty Comden (p. 66) and to Phyllis McGinley (p. 134) from
The Groucho Letters, by Groucho Marx, copyright © 1967 by
Groucho Marx, copyright renewed © 1995 by Miriam Marx,
Arthur Marx, and Melinda Marx.

Yale University Press for letters from Eugene O'Neill to
Carl Van Vechten (p. 35) and to Days Without End company
(p. 429) from *Selected Letters of Eugene O'Neill*, copyright ©
1988 by Yale University Press.

Viking Penguin, a division of Penguin Putnam Inc., for
letters from *Eighty-Four, Charing Cross Road*, by Helene
Hanff, copyright © 1970 by Helene Hanff.

Viking Penguin for a letter by James Joyce to William
Archer (28 April) from *Letters of James Joyce, Volume II*, by
James Joyce, edited by Richard Ellman, copyright © 1966,
1975 by F. Lionel Munro as Administrator of the Estate of
James Joyce.

Southern Living, Inc., for the "Dear Abigail" letter by Joe
Kropp, copyright © 1999.

Tuskegee University for a letter from George Washington
Carver to Mr. L. Robinson (January 9, 1922).

The author also wishes to thank the following friends and
correspondents or their heirs and assigns for permission to
publish their letters: Letitia Baldrige, Faith Andres Bedford,
Wendy Berndt, Elaine Greensmith Jordan, Joe Ludlow, Mary
Reilly McCall, Carolyn McKenna, Jennifer McKenzie,

Kristi McKenzie, Matthew McKenzie, Chris Medley, Stephanie Rosenbaum, the family of Jonas Salk, Lieutenant John F. Shoemaker, Maggie Stoody, Susan Thatcher, the Estate of E. B. White, and Stephanie Wiesen.

Index

OTHER BOOKS FROM
BEYOND WORDS PUBLISHING, INC.

The Secret
Author: Rhonda Byrne
$23.95, hardcover

As seen on Oprah, the groundbreaking feature length movie that revealed the great mystery of the universe, *The Secret*, is now a book, and everything you have ever wanted—unlimited joy, health, money, relationships, love, youth—is now at your very fingertips.

The Secret is an enigma that has existed throughout the history of mankind. It has been discovered, coveted, suppressed, hidden, lost, and recovered. Now for the first time The Secret is revealed to the world between the covers of this captivating book. In it you'll find all the resources you will ever need to understand and live The Secret. The book shares amazing real-life stories and testimonials of regular people who have changed their lives in profound ways. *The Secret* offers guidance on how to apply this powerful knowledge to your life in every area from health to wealth, to success and relationships, so you can obtain everything you've always wanted. No matter who you are, no matter where you are right now, no matter what you want—when you realize The Secret you can have anything.

The Power of Appreciation
The Key to a Vibrant Life
Authors: Noelle C. Nelson, Ph.D. and
Jeannine Lemare Calaba, Psy.D.
$14.95, softcover

Research confirms that when people feel appreciation, good things happen to their minds, hearts, and bodies. But appreciation is much more than a feel-good mantra. It is an actual force, an energy that can be harnessed and used to transform our daily life—relationships, work, health and aging, finances, crises, and more. *The Power of Appreciation* will open your eyes to the fabulous rewards of conscious, proactive appreciation. Based on a five-step approach to developing an appreciative mind-set, this handbook for living healthier and happier also includes tips for overcoming resistance and roadblocks, research supporting the positive effects of appreciation, and guidelines for creating an Appreciators Group.

Spiritual Writing
From Inspiration to Publication
Authors: Deborah Levine Herman with Cynthia Black
$16.95, softcover

Spiritual writers are drawn to the writing process by a powerful sense of mission. But that call to write is often at odds with the realities of publishing and the commercial needs of publishers. In *Spiritual Writing*, writer and literary agent Deborah Levine Herman and publisher Cynthia Black show writers how to create a book that both remains true to their vision and still conforms to the protocols of the publishing industry. Written with the intention of guiding and informing writers on their journey to publication, the book includes journaling exercises, tips on finding an agent and publisher, guidelines for writing query letters and proposals, a glossary of industry terms, and a comprehensive database that provides specifics on "spirit-friendly" publishers and agents.

Celebrating Time Alone
Stories of Splendid Solitude
Author: Lionel Fisher
$14.95, softcover

Celebrating Time Alone, with its profiles in solitude, shows us how to be magnificently alone through a celebration of our self: the self that can get buried under mountains of information, appointments, and activities. Lionel Fisher interviewed men and women across the country who have achieved great emotional clarity by savoring their individuality and solitude. In a writing style that is at once eloquent and down to earth, the author interweaves their real-life stories with his own insights and experiences to offer counsel, inspiration, and affirmation on living well alone.

When God Winks
How the Power of Coincidence Guides Your Life
Author: SQuire Rushnell
$16.95, hardcover

When God Winks confirms a belief secretly held by most readers: there is more to coincidences than meets the eye. Like winks from a loving grandparent, coincidences are messages from above that you are not alone and everything will be OK. The compelling theory of why coincidences exist is applied to fascinating stories in history, sports, the news, medicine, and relationships involving both everyday people and celebrities.

PowerHunch!
Living an Intuitive Life
Author: Marcia Emery, Ph.D.
Foreword: Leland Kaiser, Ph.D.
$15.95, softcover

Whether it's relationships, career, balance and healing, or simple everyday decision-making, intuition gives everyone an edge. In *PowerHunch!* Dr. Emery is your personal trainer as you develop your intuitive muscle. She shows you how to consistently and accurately apply your hunches to any problem and offers countless examples of intuition in action, covering a wide spectrum of occupations and relationships. With its intriguing stories and expert advice, *PowerHunch!* gives you the necessary tools and principles to create an intuitive life for yourself.

Forgiveness
The Greatest Healer of All
Author: Gerald G. Jampolsky, M.D.
Foreword: Neale Donald Walsch
$12.95, softcover

Forgiveness: The Greatest Healer of All is written in simple, down-to-earth language. It explains why so many of us find it difficult to forgive and why holding on to grievances is really a decision to suffer. The book describes what causes us to be unforgiving and how our minds work to justify this. It goes on to point out the toxic side effects of being unforgiving and the havoc it can play on our bodies and on our lives. But above all, it leads us to the vast benefits of forgiving.

The author shares powerful stories that open our hearts to the miracles which can take place when we truly believe that no one needs to be excluded from our love. Sprinkled throughout the book are Forgiveness Reminders that may be used as daily affirmations supporting a new life free of past grievances.

Your Authentic Self

Be Yourself at Work
Author: Ric Giardina
$14.95, softcover

Working people everywhere feel that they lead double lives: an "on the job" life and a personal life. Is it possible to live a life in which the separate parts of our personalities are united? In *Your Authentic Self*, author Ric Giardina explains that it is possible, and the key to achieving this integrated existence is authenticity. By honoring your authentic self at the workplace, you will not only be much happier, but you will also be rewarded with better on-the-job performance and more fulfilling work relationships. With straightforward techniques that produce instant results, this practical and easy-to-use guide will empower you to make the shift from seeing work as "off the path" of personal and spiritual growth to recognizing it as an integral part of your journey.

There's a Hole in My Sidewalk
The Romance of Self-Discovery
Author: Portia Nelson
$7.95, softcover

This classic, well-loved guide to life is warm, wise, and funny. Portia Nelson's book and her poem "Autobiography in Five Short Chapters" have been embraced by individuals, therapy groups, and self-help programs around the world.

To order or to request a catalog, contact
Beyond Words Publishing, Inc.
20827 N.W. Cornell Road, Suite 500
Hillsboro, OR 97124-9808
503-531-8700 or 1-800-284-9673
Visit our website at www.beyondword.com
or email us at info@beyondword.com

BEYOND WORDS

PUBLISHING

OUR CORPORATE MISSION:

Inspire to Integrity

OUR DECLARED VALUES:

We give to all of life as life has given us.

We honor all relationships.

Trust and stewardship are integral to fulfilling dreams.

Collaboration is essential to create miracles.

Creativity and aesthetics nourish the soul.

Unlimited thinking is fundamental.

Living your passion is vital.

Joy and humor open our hearts to growth.

It is important to remind ourselves of love.